The Tailgate Cookbook

THE
TAILGATE
COOKBOOK

*A Practical Handbook
of Delightful Meals for
Campers, Travelers,
and Sports Enthusiasts*

APRIL HERBERT

Galahad Books

New York

Published by arrangement with Funk & Wagnalls
Manufactured in the United States of America
DESIGNED BY VINCENT TORRE

CONTENTS

PREFACE:
A GOURMET'S
GUIDELINES

The idea of serving gourmet meals away from the convenience of home was handed to me on a silver platter. Or, more accurately, on an aluminum grill, by a slightly charred and hungry husband as he served up the hamburgers. He suggested that there might be something else, sometime, to feast on in a National Park.

That was many trips ago, and since then I have been known to serve hamburgers now and then—I love them—and have added to my repertoire Swedish Meatballs and Hawaiian Beefballs, UN Burgers and Hamburger Cassoulet, along with other meat concoctions, poultry creations, and seafood preparations.

The winter of that same year we cautiously took up skiing. That entailed a four-hour drive to the mountains and back each weekend, and we quickly tired of plain dry sandwiches. I began to experiment with transportable concoctions that would also provide more variety and nourishment before and after a weekend's hard skiing.

Next came sailing and eating aboard, station wagon "tailgate picnics," long drives to visit friends—and the idea of this cookbook, born from these experiences. Its aim is to provide gourmet meals, prepared fairly easily, while camping or boating, or fixed at home to take along driving, hiking, skating, or whatever else may lure you out of the kitchen and into the Great Outdoors.

Because the recipes are designed to cover all types of tailgate cuisine, the cookbook is arranged by activities rather than by the usual meat-poultry-fish categories. Thus Chapter 2, "Haute Cuisine and Camping Out," provides specific meals for the cook using a portable stove; Chapter 3 is for the tailgate cook who wants to barbecue his supper; while Chapters 4 and 5 take the cook back into the kitchen, preparing meals to eat en route in the car, and special dishes for various outings. The final sections include sandwiches, appetizers, salads, vegetables, bread and desserts for all the different occasions.

Common to all but a few of the recipes is the idea that exceptionally good meals can be whipped up from a simplified list of cooking ingredients and techniques. A classic dish, such as *Boeuf en Daube,* classically simmers and bubbles for hours (using up time and fuel supplies), but it can be prepared in half an hour by using a more tender cut of meat. Even "convenience foods"—canned vegetables and prepared mixes—can become part of a gourmet meal if they are cooked and seasoned with the proper touch.

I've tried to stay away from the kind of recipe that begins "Take one cup Sauce Mornay . . ." and assumes everyone has Mornay kicking around the kitchen. Instead, I've indicated at the beginning of each recipe whether it is easy, moderately easy, or time-consuming to prepare, but even the most difficult rarely takes more than half an hour. These "elaborate" recipes are such impressive dishes as Beef Wellington (page 113), which one might not think of as tailgate fare, and the reception they generally receive makes the extra effort more than worthwhile.

I've found that when you are traveling long distances, food can replenish both body and soul, while all our moods seem to worsen the hungrier we get. Last summer, after a torturous day's drive, we stopped at a seedy motel in a "godforsaken" town. "Don't" signs were everywhere, including several absolutely forbidding cooking in the rooms. The only food we had with us at that late hour was raw chicken. My husband drove off to try to find something else for us to eat. He reappeared about thirty minutes later, driving very slowly through the motel entrance, tailgate open; on it was the campstove with a sizzling filet mignon cooked to perfection. It restored my soul.

My husband and children have had other trying experiences while I researched this book—usually an author's family does not have to eat his words. My thanks to my family for putting up with a particularly varied diet, often dining on three or four of my "theories" in one meal while I tested each recipe . . . and the reader should be thankful, too, for all the recipes *not* included. As the book goes to press, it gives me pleasure to report that the children still bounce into the house after school each day echoing a refrain guaranteed to warm the heart of any cook:

"What's for dinner, Mom?"

The Tailgate Cookbook

1

STOVES, STAPLES AND SERENDIPITY

Serendipity is defined as "the gift of finding agreeable things unexpectedly." Whether or not I have that gift, many of the suggestions I offer in this chapter have come to me quite unexpectedly during my years of tailgate cooking.

For instance, I learned *not* to pack hot dogs in a narrow-necked Thermos bottle. I did it once, and while they will go in, and will stay hot, they will not come out again. Not in one piece, at least. I suggest a wide-necked thermos bottle, and perhaps a hot sauce (page 113), while you're at it.

This chapter begins with hints, gleaned from my tailgate experiences, that should prove useful to the outdoor cook. It also contains specific suggestions for equipment and food staples. Some forethought and planning in assembling these supplies can make a vacation truly a vacation.

One of the things we've encountered in our cross-country travels is the regional difference in food. Even the terms used for cuts of meat change from state to state. You can buy a "California Roast" in New York stores, and a "New York Sirloin" in Vermont, but the safest way to unscramble the labels is to know what a piece of good meat looks like. With practice one can learn to judge—by the grain, amount of fat, and price—which cut is most appropriate for each dish.

Because of these regional variations, I've included more recipes for beef and chicken than for meats that may not be readily available in some areas. For instance, we found lamb and veal to be virtually nonexistent in some parts of the South, and some special cuts, such as scallopine, were hard to come by in the West. But the regional differences can also be a boon, providing the traveler with specialties and local recipes that should not be missed—Dungenness Crab on the Coast, pompano in Florida, lobsters in Maine, for example, as well as the pick of farm fresh fruits and vegetables.

Once, while driving up the Atlantic coast, I became increasingly aware of the absence of fish in the local shops. A supermarket clerk solved the mystery for me with this classic put-down: "Why, we couldn't sell fish here, ma'am—everyone just hangs out a line and catches his own."

What makes a meal good at home will make it good in the field. There is no substitute for a fine cut of meat or a properly cooked fresh vegetable, which works to the cook's advantage, saving both time and fuel.

In line with this reasoning, I suggest using boneless steak in many recipes rather than less tender cuts of meat, thus reducing cooking time by half. Since a small amount of meat goes a long way in hearty dishes, this isn't extravagant—have you looked recently at the price tag on a package of stew meat. and noted the amount of fat you are paying for?

Since I think a good cook is adventurous by nature, most of my recipes are flexible; they do not depend on hard and fast quantities, or even definite ingredients. Many a grand meal has been the result of improvisation, and the list of staples at the end of this chapter should provide some interesting creative springboards.

A word of caution, however: the fresh air is notorious for heightening appetites, and, fortunately, their keenness. Most of the recipes are given in average amounts for four, hopefully a fresh-air foursome, but if your eaters have enormous appetites, just increase the portions of meat and potatoes, or serve a filling side dish or a rich dessert.

In addition to the recipes that are chiefly main course suggestions, there are vegetables for the campstove and grill, and many interchangeable "sidekicks"—appetizer, salad, bread and dessert ideas—to round out a meal. I leave breakfasts and most beverages to the reader's preferences, since these are mainly standard items. I do have one hint for breakfast, however: we have found that, trouble or not, bacon is a must when camping out. Otherwise the smell of bacon cooking in all the other frying pans in camp is just unbearable.

To make this cookbook as practical and efficient as possible, I have devised a new format for the recipes, making it possible to see at a glance *all* the necessary ingredients, and *all* the step-by-step cooking instructions, without constant cross-checking. To assist in meal planning, there are menu suggestions in each chapter, although other appropriate recipes may also be found in other sections of the book.

At the beginning of each recipe, I've indicated whether the dish is easy, moderate, or elaborate to prepare. This should help the cook to judge how much time will be needed to serve a dinner for the hungry lions. Even the most difficult recipes do not take long, and those to be baked at home before an outing use the oven's time, not the cook's. Many of the camping dishes can also be partially prepared ahead of time, as indicated on the recipes, so that the chief cook can have a leisurely cocktail or swim before dinner.

There are several ways to simpli. · the cook's life. Among them is a device for making canned vegetables palatable. Drain them thoroughly (leaving the can partially unopened so that the lid serves as a strainer), and then rinse them in fresh water to get rid of the tinny flavor. Another is to use whole amounts of an ingredient whenever possible, and avoid packing up half-used cans. Or plan a meal so that an ingredient is used for two recipes. Buy

a pint of sour cream, for instance, and use some of it to make a
dip for potato chips and stir the rest into a sauce for Swedish
Meatballs.

Good planning can be a great advantage too. By balancing a
heavy entrée with light vegetable appetizers, the cook provides
needed vitamins, while an assortment of cheese and fruit for
dessert can be a welcome supplement to a starchy main course.

A more particular problem is the dieter faced with bread,
bread, BREAD on a long trip. Since this is my perennial plight,
I've devised ways to feed the family well without sending my
calorie count sky high. One is to make the usual sandwich, but
use thin-sliced bread and serve it open-faced to the dieter (throw-
ing that unused slice of bread to the seagulls). Another way is to
substitute cottage cheese for mayonnaise or butter, flavoring it
with spices, onions, or mushrooms.

My favorite way is to make "no-bread sandwiches," using
celery sticks, hollowed-out tomatoes, green peppers, or cucumber
boats to hold the fillings. The only real dieting problem on a tailgate menu (besides one's appetite) is that breadless foods can be
harder to pack—but suggestions for this follow, along with all the
other equipment needed for tailgate cuisine.

EQUIPMENT

There is an endless variety of equipment available for all budgets
and occasions, ranging from a simple wicker picnic basket to a
portable bar with a crystal service for six. New items—and gim-
micks—appear almost daily as more and more people take up the
mobile life. The tailgate cook should be able to choose the best in
terms of cost and comfort.

The equipment needed will, of course, depend on the kind of
outing involved. Therefore, the list at the end of this section is
divided into items necessary for picnicking, cooking on a portable
stove, and barbecuing, whether on a special outing or a camp trip.

If you're going to buy new equipment for any kind of tailgate meals, take the time to look at the wide—and wild—variety of items now available. There are some beautiful designs in decorated paper goods, plastic containers, bright enamelware, even pots and pans. To further enhance a well-cooked meal, I have found it pleases me to select a basic color scheme and try to find bright items to match it. We have a collection of blue and green enamel mugs and plates, and a blue plastic bin for storing our cutlery—all very inexpensive and durable—which I match with decorated paper napkins and cups.

For the most up-to-the-minute, ingenious (and often expensive) equipment, a trip to Abercrombie & Fitch (at Madison Avenue and 45th Street, New York, N.Y. 10017) or Hammacher Schlemmer (147 East 57th Street, New York, N.Y 10022) can set one to drooling. For out-of-towners, their catalogues include a range of incredible devices, including a portable plastic sink ("Campteen," at Abercrombie's); a baking oven (with thermometer) to use over a campstove, toasters for same, and even plastic egg carriers!

With such a wide range of price, size, and efficiency in equipment, it's wise to shop around for the best buys. Look for compactness, ease of operation and cleaning, and durability. Choose one kind of fuel to power all of your appliances. (We're partial to propane gas equipment, because it's safe and easy to pack.)

Whether outfitting the car for camping or picnics, try to buy containers that will fit in as neatly and tightly as possible—an ice chest, for instance, that sits snugly on top of the campstove while traveling, a sturdy carton to hold staples, small nesting plastic boxes for special diet foods and salads. Square containers use less space than round, though we also make use of empty coffee cans, glass jars, and aluminum foil pans for storing and packing foods (e.g. the dieter's no-bread sandwiches.)

For all our tailgate trips, we have a small thermal chest which we keep in the front of the car to hold Cokes and lunch or a picnic from home. Ours is finished in a dapper blue-green check, and can hold two six-packs and a stick of celery, or—more practically—one six-pack, our sandwiches, and a plastic bag of ice.

Whichever kind of ice chest is used, there are ways to increase its efficiency. Ice lasts longer if bought by the block, with the excess water drained frequently. The chest operates more efficiently when it is tightly packed, with items stored in the order in which they will be used. There are two ways to keep foods dry: (1) wrap the ice in a plastic bag; (2) use containers, such as coffee cans (the type with reclosable lids) to hold butter, cold cuts, cheeses, etc.

Once you've assembled all the equipment needed for picnicking or camping, keep it together in one storage space at home. Have everything handy. Packing goes much faster, and essentials are less likely to be forgotten, if you do.

Our car's glove compartment always contains: a bottle opener, a small paring knife (to divvy up the last cookie), a box of Kleenex (to use when you've forgotten the napkins), road maps and, from now on, a copy of this cookbook.

PICNICKING: Quart size wide-mouth thermos bottles

Half-gallon wide-mouth thermos bottle (for soups, chowders, punches)

Beer-can opener, corkscrew, paring knife

Plastic forks, spoons

Paper plates, napkins, cups (make sure they're "hot cups" if serving soups or coffee)

Kleenex, Wash 'n Dries

Small ice chest and/or picnic basket

Assortment of plastic containers with tight lids, jars, aluminum foil pans (saved from frozen foods), plastic bags; ties and tape to seal foods

Fondue set with forks and cooking fuel—optional, but marvelous for a Grand Occasion.

CAMPING: Thermos bottles, as above

Rigid portable ice chest, big enough to hold block ice and perishables

Small insulated carrier, handy for lunches, cold drinks while driving

Campstove: compact two-burner propane gas

model recommended (about the size of an attaché case)

Extra fuel—especially if using propane gas, since it's difficult to tell when supply gets low

Metal, enamel, or plastic tableware: plates, mugs, bowls (handy for mixing, and for cereals and salads)

Plastic glasses or paper cups

Flatware: one setting per person (I use steak knives to double as parers and soup spoons to double as servers)

Cooking utensils: carving knife and fork, spatula, tongs, spoon, strainer

Pot-holders, measuring cup

Pots and pans: best are complete nesting sets (some now come with a Teflon-coated frying pan); an extra, very large frying pan (optional, but highly recommended if cooking for more than two)

Can openers: beer-can type and regular can type

Empty two-pound coffee can with lid, for storing cold cuts, butter, cheese

Ice pick, corkscrew

Matches—without which, forget everything else!

BARBECUING:
(Charcoal
Cooking)

Matches, utensils, openers, place settings, as listed above

Sandwich grill, metal or bamboo skewers

Charcoal, newspapers, and kindling (or instant fire starter)

Non-culinary reminders to make meals more pleasant: flashlights, Band-Aids, bug spray.

STAPLES

The difference between an ordinary dinner and a gourmet repast is not necessarily determined by price or effort, but more subtly by proper treatment and flavoring. While we try to keep to a minimum the amount of food we take along on our camping trips, there are many extras that take up little space and add immeasurably to our enjoyment. A small bottle of soy sauce and a baby-food jar of cornstarch can unfold the wonders of the Orient; a jar of mushrooms, a clove of garlic, and a bottle of wine hold out the promise of exquisite French cuisine—and, should all else fail, the wine will serve to soothe the discouraged cook and the disgruntled guests.

While there should be no problem in assembling staples for recipes prepared at home, space is at a premium when traveling. You will find, despite advertising claims, that economy-sized packages are not the best buys. I get the smallest sizes in most things. I buy shaker packages of salt, pepper, sugar, and flour, or I transport the staples in plastic bags, spice bottles, or leftover jars.

Since the following list is meant to be comprehensive it should be amended to suit the needs of your family. Your own taste buds will tell you which staples are worth the space. As a rule, if it's an item you don't use at home, you probably won't use it when you are camping—but then again, it might be fun to try something new.

STAPLE ITEMS: Sugar, salt, pepper (coarse grain preferred)
Flour, cornstarch (in small jars or plastic bags)
Garlic, garlic salt, fresh onions, instant onion
Bouillon cubes or instant bouillon (beef and/or chicken)
Spices: cinnamon, nutmeg or ginger; tarragon, basil or chervil; marjoram or thyme; oregano, curry powder, dill weed, parsley, chives, chili powder
Coffee, tea, cocoa, milk
Butter, eggs, bread, bacon (save bacon fat for cooking)
Mayonnaise, ketchup, mustard, soy sauce

Olive oil (with screw cap) and wine vinegar, or
bottled salad dressing and cooking oil

Peanut butter, jam or jelly (currant and grape
jelly are also useful for thickening sauces)

Crackers (can be crushed and used in place of
bread crumbs)

Wine, dry red and/or white; miniature bottles of
sherry and/or brandy

Instant iced tea, instant coffee, Kool-Aid, orange
concentrate, soft drinks, beer

HANDY TO
HAVE ON HAND
(or buy as
the recipe
demands):

Grated Parmesan cheese; blue cheese, Swiss,
Muenster or cheddar

Worcestershire sauce, A-1 sauce, relish, bottled
Hollandaise sauce

Capers, chutney, horseradish, anchovy paste

Brown sugar, honey

Sour cream, instant whipped cream

Bottled lemon juice or fresh lemons and/or limes

Bread crumbs, biscuit mix, cereals, rice, canned
potatoes, spaghetti or noodles

Canned tomatoes, tomato sauce or tomato paste

Raisins, pickles, nuts (for hors d'oeuvres and
cooking)

Canned tuna, mushrooms, soups, onion rings

AND SOME
INEDIBLES:

Paper towels, aluminum foil, plastic bags

Soap, soap-pads, plastic garbage bags

2

HAUTE CUISINE
AND CAMPING OUT

Since it is my basic belief that one can find gastronomic delight in the depths of the forest, this chapter is really devoted to the camping cook—whether home is a tent, a trailer, or a sleeping bag. I have not, however, planned the recipes for the backwoodsman hunter (I can barely bring myself to slap a mosquito), nor for a backwoods portage where everything must be canned or dehydrated. By substituting dried meats and vegetables, many of the recipes could be adapted miles from civilization, but it is not my intention to take the cook away from the tailgate for any length of time.

Most of the recipes given here are simplified versions of classic dishes, though some are the result of fanciful flights of my imagination. Not having complete trust in my own taste buds, I've had the more fanciful creations tested by friends on their families, and have retained only the yeas and hurrays. (One taste-tester friend reported that the recipes worked just as well at home as at dockside, thus providing her with a whole new set of quickly prepared family meals.)

For most of the dishes in this section, I've tried to make the entrée a substantial one, needing perhaps a salad or bread to complete the main course. I have an aversion to scrubbing pots and pans anywhere, and most especially in a cold-running brook.

Therefore, many of the recipes will need only one burner, none more than two.

Besides simplifying the preparation of meals, I've found ways to make it easier to wash up afterwards. I make use of paper plates whenever possible for chopping vegetables, to dredge meat in bread crumbs or flour, and to hold the first batch of meatballs while browning the next. Paper cups are also useful for measuring and mixing ingredients (e.g., if you fill a five-ounce paper cup to about a half inch from the top, you have eight tablespoons, four ounces, or one-half cup measured accurately enough for any recipe).

Marketing is a time-consuming activity, especially when you have just driven many miles to a campsite. To make it easier, I've used a recipe format that shows the necessary ingredients at a glance. Many of the staple items will already be at hand and many can be freely substituted for other similar foods.

Another way to make life easier on a camping trip is to partially prepare meals ahead of time, allowing flavors to blend in the pot while the cook has a swim or a cocktail. Whenever this is possible, I've indicated which steps can be completed beforehand. Even with recipes which have to be cooked at the last minute, such as Sukiyaki, the chef can assemble and prepare all the ingredients at leisure during the day, wrapping them in foil until suppertime.

Remember, almost anything that can be cooked on top of the stove at home can be produced on a campstove, and there's nothing to prevent your simplifying family favorites and trying them outdoors. The following recipes provide a wide variety of ideas, from inexpensive and filling meal-in-a-pot suppers to truly Grand Dinners (some of which are also surprisingly inexpensive).

MENU SUGGESTIONS

(Recipes marked * are included in this book; others are store-bought, standard items.)

Liver Paté (canned) and Crackers
Steak on Giant Croutons*
Mushrooms and Sour Cream*
Sautéed Bananas*

*

Caviar Dip* and Potato Chips
Swedish Meatballs*
Noodles
Cucumber Dill Salad*
Cookies

*

Breadsticks, Carrots, and Celery
Veal Niçoise*
Rolls
Artichoke Hearts and Peas*
Liqueured Fruits*

*

Cherry Tomatoes and Pickle Spears
Sweet and Pungent Pork*
Fried Rice (canned)
Fortune Cookies

*

Baby Shrimp Hors d'Oeuvres*
Chicken and Grapes*
French Bread
Dilled Zucchini*
Instant Strawberry Shortcake*

*

Steak Tartare in Mushroom Caps*
Sautéed Oysters*
Giant Croutons*
Asparagus Salad*
Apricots with Jam*

*

Melon and Prosciutto*
Paella*
Ambrosia Cup*

*

Brandied Blue Cheese* and Crackers
One Pot Spaghetti*
Onion Tomato Salad*
Strawberries in Wine*

Sukiyaki

EASY TO DO: aside from its marvelous flavor and low calorie
count, Sukiyaki, is readily adaptable for use with a variety of
vegetables. It must be cooked very fast, so be sure to have both
the ingredients and the diners ready beforehand.

To prepare ahead of time or just before serving:

SLICE: *1 lb. boneless steak* (inexpensive cut), in thin
             strips
             3 onions, as thin as possible
             ¼ lb. mushrooms, ¼ inch thick
             1 green pepper (or 1 cucumber) in thin strips
             4 scallions (optional), into coarse, diagonal
             pieces

1 pkg. (10 oz.) spinach, trimmed (or 1 16-oz. can bean sprouts, drained)

Before serving:

SAUTÉ: Meat and onions in:
                  2 Tbs. bacon fat (or oil), very quickly

ADD: Sliced vegetables
                  ½ cup soy sauce
                  ½ cup white wine (or water)

STIR-FRY: Over very high heat till vegetables are just barely cooked and still retain color—about 5 minutes

SERVE WITH: Boiled rice

Serves 4

• •

Steak Diane

EASY TO DO: this magnificent dish is both easy and expensive, since it must be made with fine quality beef. I try to save it to serve when our spirits are low, and then watch them soar!

CREAM: *½ stick butter* with:
                  4 Tbs. chives (fresh or freeze-dried). Set aside

TRIM: *4 portions first-rate boneless steak* (club, filets, or boned sirloin) and secure with toothpicks if needed

SAUTÉ IN: *2 Tbs. butter* over fairly high heat until done to your taste—this will be very fast. Turn off heat

ADD: 1 Tb. chive-butter, on top of each steak

ADD TO PAN: *4 Tbs. sherry,* swirling pan to dissolve juices;
                 spoon over chive-butter to melt slightly

SERVE: Immediately, with tossed green salad and Garlic
                 Bread (p. 175)

Serves 4

• •

Oriental Steak

MODERATE TIME: an inexpensive cut of steak is transformed in
this adaptation of a Chinese dish.

Can be prepared ahead of time:

SLICE: *1½ lbs. boneless steak* (top round, flank, etc.)
                 across grain into long, thin strips

SAUTÉ IN: *2 Tbs. olive oil* (or bacon fat)
                 1 clove garlic, minced
                 ½ tsp. ginger (optional), on very high heat, till
                 seared

ADD: *4 Tbs. soy sauce*
                 1 tsp. sugar
                 2 tomatoes, cut in chunks
                 2 green peppers, cut in chunks
                 1 can (16 oz.) bean sprouts, drained

SIMMER: 10 minutes, covered

Before serving:

ADD: *1 Tb. cornstarch,* mixed with
                 4 Tbs. water, and stir on high heat till thick-
                 ened

SERVE WITH: Chinese Fried Rice (1 can)

Serves 4

● ●

Steak on Giant Croutons

EASY TO DO: another exquisite, expensive, rich and easy dinner, but be sure to have plenty of butter on hand for it.

CREAM: *4 Tbs. butter,* at room temperature, with
                2 Tbs. chopped parsley. Set aside

SAUTÉ: *4 slices white bread* in
                4 Tbs. butter, two tablespoons for each side, till lightly browned. Wrap in aluminum foil to keep warm and set aside

SAUTÉ: *4 portions club steak,* well trimmed, in
                1 Tb. butter over fairly high heat till done to your taste

ADD: 1½ Tbs. parsley-butter to each steak, place steaks on croutons

ADD TO PAN: *2–4 Tbs. wine* (red or white), stir briefly and spoon over steaks

SERVE WITH: Spinach Salad (p. 165)

Serves 4

● ●

Steak Piccanté

EASY TO DO: best done for two, while the children are off roasting wieners at a bonfire.

TRIM:	*1 club steak,* ¾ inches thick, trimmed and cut in half
SEASON WITH:	*1 tsp. garlic salt*
SAUTÉ IN:	*2 Tbs. butter,* very hot, to sear both sides, then moderate heat till cooked to your taste; remove to serving plates, and turn off heat
ADD TO PAN:	*Juice of 1 lemon* *2–3 Tbs. Madeira* (or dry white wine). Tilt pan to dissolve juices and pour over steak
SERVE WITH:	French bread and salad

Serves 2

• •

Boeuf en Daube

EASY TO DO: a meal-in-one, quickly prepared by using an inexpensive cut of boneless steak rather than stew meat.

Can be prepared ahead of time and reheated:

SAUTÉ:	*1½ lbs. boneless steak,* sliced thin and *2 onions,* sliced thin, in: *1 Tb. bacon fat* (or oil), over fairly high flame
ADD:	*1 cup red wine,* and reduce heat
ADD:	*1 can (8 oz.) baby carrots* *1 can (16 oz.) whole new potatoes,* drained and rinsed

Rind of 1 orange, grated
½ tsp. each pepper, garlic salt, nutmeg, thyme
  (or combination of other spices such as marjoram and cinnamon or ginger)

SIMMER: 15 minutes, covered

Serves 4

• •

Beef Stroganoff

MODERATE TIME: slicing the meat into very thin pieces makes the
dish tender and tasty.

Can be prepared ahead of time:

SLICE: 1½ lbs. boneless steak (inexpensive cut) into
                     very thin strips

SAUTÉ: 2 onions, sliced thin, in:
                     2 Tbs. butter, over high heat; push to side

ADD AND
BROWN: Sliced meat, turning quickly; reduce heat

ADD: 1 cup water
                     1 beef bouillon cube (or 1 Tb. instant bouillon)
                     1 tsp. prepared mustard
                     1 tsp. grated lemon rind
                     Garlic salt, pepper to taste

SIMMER: 10 minutes, covered

Before serving:

STIR IN: ½ pt. sour cream, and heat but do not let boil

SERVE WITH: Buttered noodles or rice and salad

Serves 4

• •

Mock Sauerbraten

MODERATE TIME: a completely unauthentic version of the classic German specialty.

Can be prepared ahead of time:

SAUTÉ:	1½ *lbs. boneless steak,* cut in thin strips, in:
	2 *Tbs. bacon fat* (or oil), until browned
SPRINKLE	1 *Tb. flour*
WITH:	4 *Tbs. instant minced onion*
	Salt, pepper, to taste; reduce heat
ADD:	½ *cup water*
	1 *Tb. sugar*
	½ *cup vinegar*
	1 *tsp. nutmeg* (or cinnamon)
SIMMER:	½ hour, covered

Before serving:

ADD:	6 *gingersnap cookies,* crushed, and stir over low heat until sauce is thickened

Serves 4

• •

Swedish Meatballs

MODERATE TIME: the meatballs are so soft and juicy that they must be turned carefully.

Can be prepared ahead of time:

MIX:	1 *egg,* beaten with a fork
	1 *lb. chopped beef*

½ cup bread crumbs
¾ cup milk
1 Tb. instant minced onion
½ tsp. each garlic salt, pepper, nutmeg (or
    cinnamon)

SHAPE INTO: Large meatballs (almost 2-inch diameter)

BROWN IN: 1 Tb. butter, lower heat. It is easier to brown
               half the meatballs at a time, and remove to a
               paper plate

ADD: 1 cup bouillon, chicken or beef (or half bouillon,
               half wine; or 1 cup water plus 1 bouillon
               cube or 1 tsp. instant bouillon) and stir to
               loosen any meat particles in pan

SIMMER: 20 minutes, covered

Before serving:

REHEAT   ½ cup sour cream
AND ADD: 1 Tb. dill, fresh or dried
               1 tsp. grated lemon (optional)

SERVE WITH: Buttered noodles or rice and salad

Serves 4

• •

Hawaiian Beefballs

MODERATE TIME: a very tasty, and very inexpensive, family or
party dish.

Can be prepared ahead of time:

MIX: 1½ lbs. ground beef
               1 egg, beaten with fork
               Salt, pepper, to taste; shape into 1-inch meat-
                  balls

BROWN IN: *1 Tb. olive oil,* pouring off excess fat

ADD: *¾ cup chicken bouillon* (or white wine;
                    or ¾ cup water plus 1 bouillon cube
                    2 cans (8¼ ozs.) pineapple chunks, reserving
                    juice
                    2 green peppers, cut in thin strips

SIMMER: 10 minutes, covered

MIX: *1 Tb. cornstarch*
                    2 Tbs. soy sauce
                    4 Tbs. vinegar
                    ¼ cup reserved pineapple juice

Before serving:
Reheat, if done ahead

ADD: Cornstarch mixture and stir, on high heat, till
                    thickened

SERVE WITH: Chow Mein Noodles (1 can) or boiled rice

Serves 4

● ●

Mediterranean Dinner

MODERATE TIME: exotic flavors bring to mind food from the Near
Eastern shores.

Can be prepared ahead of time and reheated:

SAUTÉ: *1 onion,* chopped coarsely, in:
                    1 Tb. olive oil; push to side of pan

ADD: *1 lb. ground beef,* and brown quickly, pouring
                    off excess fat

ADD:	½ cup red wine
	1 cup water
	1 cup raisins
	½ cup pine nuts (or chopped cashews if pine nuts are not available)
	1 tsp. nutmeg (or curry for a completely different flavor)
SIMMER:	15 minutes, covered
STIR IN:	¼ cup pine nuts
	2 Tbs. chopped parsley
SERVE WITH:	Boiled rice and Artichoke Salad (p. 159)

Serves 4

• •

Salt-Fried Hamburgers

EASY TO DO: this method of cooking sears the meat without using extra fat, and works equally well with small steaks and chops.

SPRINKLE:	1–2 tsps. garlic salt (or salt) in frying pan, and place on very high heat until salt begins to brown
ADD:	4 large hamburger patties, and sear on both sides; lower heat and cook to desired doneness
SERVE WITH:	Mushroom Sauce or Cheese Sauce if desired

Serves 4

• •

Mushroom Sauce

Can be prepared ahead of time and reheated:

SAUTÉ: *1 shallot* (or 2 scallions), chopped fine
              3 Tbs. chopped parsley, in:
              3 Tbs. butter, until just wilted

ADD: ¼ *lb. mushrooms,* chopped coarsely, and cook
              till done

ADD: ¼ *cup red wine,* and cook 10 minutes, uncovered

Serves 4

• •

Cheese Sauce

EASY TO DO: the sauce makes this a tempting meal, but it must
be made just before—or while—cooking the hamburgers, and
served at once.

MELT: *1½ Tbs. butter* over very low heat

STIR IN: *1 Tb. flour*
              ½ *cup milk,* added gradually
              Dash garlic salt, pepper, Worcestershire sauce,
              and cook until hot but not boiling

ADD: *4 ozs. cheddar cheese,* slivered, stir constantly
              and remove from heat as soon as cheese is
              melted

Serves 4

• •

Hamburger Grinders

EASY TO DO: wedges, heroes, submarines—the kids will know what they're called and how to gobble them up.

Can be prepared ahead of time and reheated:

SAUTÉ:	*2 onions,* chopped coarsely, in: *4 Tbs. olive oil,* brown lightly and push to side
ADD:	*1 lb. chopped beef,* break into small pieces with a fork and cook over fairly high heat
ADD:	*1 can (8 oz.) tomato sauce* *½ cup red wine* *1 tsp. each oregano, chopped parsley, and garlic salt*
SIMMER:	10 minutes, uncovered, over very low heat
SERVE ON:	*4 large Grinder Rolls* (or 1 loaf Italian Bread), sliced lengthwise

Serves 4

•   •

Chili Tortillas

EASY TO DO: the Southwest's answer to the Hot Dog Stand.

Can be prepared ahead of time and reheated:

SAUTÉ:	*1 lb. chopped beef* *2 Tbs. instant minced onion* in: *1 Tb. olive oil,* draining off excess fat
ADD:	*6 ozs. (½ bottle) chili sauce, or more to taste* *2 Tbs. red wine (optional)*

SIMMER: 10 minutes

SERVE ON: *Tortillas* (canned) or hamburger buns

TOP WITH: *Grated Parmesan cheese (optional)*
                   Shredded lettuce (optional)

Serves 4

• •

Veal Scallopine with White Wine

EASY TO DO: the delicate flavor is especially welcome on a warm
summer evening.

DREDGE: *4 large veal scallopine* in:
                   2 Tbs. flour (on paper plate, of course)

SAUTÉ IN: *3 Tbs. butter* until lightly browned on each side

ADD: *½ cup dry white wine*
                   1 can (6 oz.) button mushrooms

SIMMER: 10 minutes, uncovered

SERVE WITH: Butter Rolls (for the sauce) and Asparagus
                   Salad (p. 159)

Serves 4

N.B. Wiener Schnitzel, suggested as a cold dish (p. 100), is another way of preparing veal scallopine, and tastes even better
served hot.

• •

Swirled Veal Chops

EASY TO DO: what I call the "butter-swirl" method of cooking works wonders with lean hamburgers, lamb-chops and minute steaks.

Can be prepared ahead of time:

SAUTÉ:	*4 large veal chops* in:
	2 Tbs. butter, till lightly browned on each side
ADD:	*¼ cup white wine,* and reduce heat
SIMMER:	30 minutes, covered, adding more wine if needed
CREAM:	*4 Tbs. butter* with:
	2 Tbs. parsley and /or chives

Before serving:

REHEAT:	Chops and sauce
ADD:	1 Tb. of the creamed butter mixture to each chop, swirl sauce in pan and spoon just enough over chops to warm creamed butter
SERVE WITH:	Noodles and Boston Lettuce Salad (p. 160)

Serves 4

• •

Veal Niçoise

EASY TO DO: a fast and delicious adaptation of a classic dish.

Can be prepared ahead of time and reheated:

SLICE:	*1¼ lbs. boneless veal* into small, thin pieces

SPRINKLE WITH:	*1 Tb. flour*
SAUTÉ IN:	*2 Tbs. olive oil,* seasoned with *Garlic salt,* till veal is lightly browned
ADD:	*½ cup dry white wine,* and reduce heat
SIMMER:	15 minutes, covered
ADD:	*1 tsp. anchovy paste* *¼ cup chopped parsley* *1 tsp. fresh lemon juice (optional)* More wine if sauce is too thick
STIR:	Until hot and blended
SERVE WITH:	Biscuits or noodles and salad

Serves 4

• •

Veal Ragout

MODERATE TIME: this dish uses a less expensive cut of veal, but you must allow more time to let it simmer and become tender.

Can be prepared ahead of time:

SLICE:	*1½ lbs. boneless veal roast* into small, thin pieces
SPRINKLE WITH:	*2 Tbs. lemon juice* (preferably fresh) *2 Tbs. dry white wine* *2 Tbs. flour*
SAUTÉ IN:	*1½ Tbs. butter,* till lightly browned
ADD:	*½ cup dry white wine,* and reduce heat
SIMMER:	45 minutes, covered

Before serving:

ADD: ½ *lb. mushrooms,* sliced thin, and cook 5 minutes

SERVE WITH: Boiled rice and Cucumber Dill Salad (p. 160)

Serves 4

• •

Lamburgers

EASY TO DO: these provide the flavor of lamb without the expense
of chops.

Can be prepared ahead of time:

MIX: 1 *lb. ground lamb* (or 4 patties, available in
                     many supermarkets)
                     1 *Tbs. instant minced onion*
                     1 *egg,* beaten with a fork
                     ½ *cup bread crumbs*
                     2 *Tbs. chopped mint* (or 1 Tb. dried mint)
                     2 *sprigs parsley,* chopped fine

FORM: 4 patties

Before serving:

HEAT: 2 *Tbs. olive oil* (or bacon fat), and sear patties;
                     reduce heat and cook about 10 minutes, to de-
                     sired doneness

SERVE WITH: Sourdough bread

Serves 4

• •

Sweet and Pungent Pork

ELABORATE: this superb meal takes time, unless you can find a butcher willing to cut and trim the meat.

Can be prepared ahead of time:

MIX:
1 clove garlic, minced
1 tsp. salt
2 Tbs. olive oil, in large skillet, over high heat

ADD:
1¼ lbs. boneless pork, trimmed and cut into 1-inch cubes

SPRINKLE WITH:
2 Tbs. flour, and brown quickly on all sides

ADD:
⅓ cup chicken bouillon (dissolve 1 bouillon cube in 1 cup of hot water and reserve ⅔ cup)
1 can (8¼ oz.) pineapple chunks, drained
2 green peppers, cut in thin strips

SIMMER:
10 minutes, covered

Before serving:

REHEAT AND ADD:
2 Tbs. cornstarch, mixed with:
1 Tb. soy sauce
6 Tbs. each vinegar and sugar
⅔ cup bouillon, and stir till thickened

SERVE WITH:
Boiled rice

Serves 4

• •

Pork Chops with Raisins

Easy To Do: raisins and orange juice complement the flavor of
pork perfectly.

Can be prepared ahead of time and reheated:

SAUTÉ: *4 large pork chops* in:
                    1 Tb. butter, till brown on both sides

ADD: *1 cup orange juice* (frozen or bottled)
                    1 cup raisins
                    1 orange, juice and grated rind (optional)

SIMMER: ½ hour, covered, or until chops are well done

SERVE WITH: Chinese Fried Rice (1 can) and salad

Serves 4

• •

Pork and Apples

Easy To Do: fried apples always seem to win special applause
from the children.

SAUTÉ: *4 large pork chops,* until well browned, discard-
                    ing any excess fat; stack at side of pan

ADD: *4 Tbs. butter*
                    4 large apples (tart are best), cored and sliced

SAUTÉ: 5 minutes, or until brown on both sides, and re-
                    place chops among the apples

SIMMER: 20 minutes, covered, or until chops are well done

SERVE WITH: *Cinnamon (optional)* to sprinkle on apples

Variation: Substitute pork sausages for chops

Serves 4

• •

Glazed Pork Chops

MODERATE TIME: a little extra time makes this a most attractive dish.

SAUTÉ: *4 large pork chops,* trimmed of fat, in:
                   1 Tb. butter, till browned on both sides

ADD: *¾ cup cider* (or sherry), and reduce heat

SIMMER: 30 minutes, covered, or until well done

SPREAD: *Currant jelly* over chops, and gently spoon
                   sauce over jelly to glaze

SERVE WITH: French bread and Spinach Salad (p. 165)

Serves 4

• •

Ham and Bananas

EASY TO DO: use a cut of precooked, ready-to-eat ham, and this dinner will be ready in a jiffy.

SAUTÉ: *1½ lbs. ham steak* in:
                   2 Tbs. butter, and set aside

ADD: *2 Tbs. butter* (more if necessary)
                   4 bananas, halved lengthwise, and fry till lightly
                   browned on both sides

SPRINKLE   *4 Tbs. brown sugar*
WITH: *Juice of half a lemon*

Serves 4

• •

Ham and Pineapple

EASY TO DO: substitute *two cans (8¼ oz. each) sliced pineapple,* and ½ cup of the pineapple syrup for the bananas and lemon juice in the above recipe.

Serves 4

• •

Jambalaya

MODERATE TIME: a marvelous combination of flavors, and only one pot to wash.

SAUTÉ:	*1 medium onion,* chopped fine *1 green pepper,* chopped fine *1 clove garlic,* minced, in: *4 Tbs. olive oil* (or butter), till golden
ADD:	*1 pkg. (8 oz.) shrimp,* thawed (or 1 can) *1 cup cooked ham* (or Canadian Bacon), diced, and cook 2 minutes
ADD:	*1 can (1 lb. 12 oz.) plum tomatoes,* undrained *½ cup white wine* *½ cup water* *Salt, pepper, oregano* to taste, and bring to boil
ADD:	*1 cup uncooked rice,* and reduce heat.
SIMMER:	½ hour, covered, stirring occasionally, until rice is tender and liquid is absorbed. If instant rice is used, simmer only 10 minutes
SERVE WITH:	Artichoke Salad (p. 159)

Serves 4

• •

Coq au Vin

MODERATE TIME: a family favorite, this version not only has a chicken in every pot, but the vegetables and potatoes too.

Can be prepared ahead of time and reheated:

SAUTÉ:	*1 frying chicken,* cut up (or *2 split chicken breasts*), in:
	4 Tbs. butter, until golden on all sides; push aside
ADD:	*1 large onion,* chopped fine, and brown lightly
ADD:	*1 cup dry wine* (red or white), reduce heat and stir to dissolve drippings in pan
ADD:	*1 tsp. each garlic salt, pepper, thyme, marjoram*
	1 can (8 oz.) baby carrots, rinsed and drained
	1 can (1 lb.) new potatoes, rinsed and drained
	1 can (8 oz.) mushrooms, drained
SIMMER:	20 minutes, covered
SERVE WITH:	French bread and wine, to be authentic!

Serves 4

• •

Poulet Marengo

MODERATE TIME: truly a "company's coming" dinner if lobster meat is included, but very good even without it.

Can be prepared ahead of time:

SAUTÉ:	*2 chicken breasts,* split, in:
	2 Tbs. butter, till lightly browned. Reduce heat

ADD: *1 Tb. flour,* stirring into juices

1 cup dry white wine, stirring till slightly thickened

1 can (8 oz.) mushrooms, drained

½ tsp. garlic salt, pepper

2 Tbs. dried chives

SIMMER: 20 minutes, covered

Before serving:

ADD: *2 fresh tomatoes,* cut into chunks

1 can (5 oz.) lobster meat (optional)

SIMMER: 5 minutes, uncovered

SERVE WITH: Boiled new potatoes and salad

Serves 4

• •

Chicken Cacciatore

MODERATE TIME: the Italian flavoring tastes particularly good on a cool evening.

Can be prepared ahead of time:

SAUTÉ: *1 frying chicken,* cut up, in:

4 Tbs. olive oil, until browned

ADD: *1 clove garlic,* minced

1 tsp. each garlic salt, thyme, oregano

1 can (1 lb. 12 oz.) plum tomatoes

1 green pepper, chopped

1 cup dry wine (red or white) bring to boil and reduce heat

SIMMER: 30 minutes, covered

Before serving:

ADD: ½ *lb. mushooms,* sliced (or 8 oz. canned mush-
                rooms), and cook 10 minutes, uncovered

SERVE WITH: Italian bread and salad

Serves 4

• •

Chicken and Grapes

EASY To Do: delightfully quick and refreshing, this is a marvelous dish for company when doubled or even quadrupled.

Can be prepared ahead of time:

SAUTÉ: *2 large chicken breasts,* boned, split and skinned,
                in:
                2 Tbs. butter, till golden

ADD: ¾ *cup dry white wine,* stirring to dissolve pan
                juices, and reduce heat

SIMMER: 10 minutes, covered

Before serving:

ADD: *1 bunch seedless grapes*
                ½ *cup chopped nuts (optional)*

SIMMER: 10 minutes, covered

SERVE WITH: Butter rolls, rice or noodles, to take advantage
                of the sauce

Serves 4—if cooking for more, reduce the ratio of wine to
    chicken somewhat.

• •

Chicken and Artichokes

MODERATE TIME: the delicious flavor combinations are equally
appropriate for a family or a company dinner.

Can be prepared ahead of time and reheated:

SAUTÉ: *2 large chicken breasts,* split, in:
                2 Tbs. butter, over fairly high heat, until lightly
                    browned on both sides

ADD: *2 Tbs. chopped shallots* (or 1 scallion)
                1 clove garlic, minced, and stir to brown lightly

ADD: *¾ cup white wine* (or chicken bouillon)
                1 can (15 oz.) artichoke hearts, packed in water,
                    drained and rinsed

SIMMER: 20 minutes, covered, stirring once

SERVE WITH: Cold Rice Salad (p. 168)

Serves 4

• •

Glazed Chicken

MODERATE TIME: the versatile chicken appears in Oriental garb
this time.

Can be prepared ahead of time:

SAUTÉ: *1 frying chicken,* cut up, in:
                2 Tbs. olive oil, seasoned with:
                1 tsp. each ginger, salt, pepper, till browned

ADD:	½–¾ cup water
	4 Tbs. soy sauce
	1 Tb. lemon juice (optional), stir and reduce heat
SIMMER:	20–30 minutes, covered, until· chicken is just done

Before serving:

MIX:	2 Tbs. cornstarch
	2 Tbs. water, and add to chicken
SIMMER:	Uncovered, stirring until sauce is thickened
SERVE WITH:	Boiled rice

Serves 4

• •

Chicken with Paté

EASY TO DO: use a good, imported paté in this dish, and serve any extra for hors d'oeuvres.

SAUTÉ:	2 large chicken breasts, boned, split and skinned, in:
	4 Tbs. butter, until golden on both sides
ADD:	½ cup dry white wine, and reduce heat
SIMMER:	10–15 minutes, covered, until chicken is done
ADD:	4 slices paté (canned), placing one slice on top of each breast
	2 Tbs. sherry (optional)
	1 Tb. butter, swirl in pan and spoon sauce over paté until paté is warmed
SERVE WITH:	Giant Croutons (p. 173) or French bread

Serves 4

• •

Paella

ELABORATE: this Spanish dish takes about twenty minutes to prepare and twenty minutes to cook, and makes a meal-in-one-dish feast.

SAUTÉ:
1 medium onion, chopped fine
1 garlic clove, minced, in:
3 Tbs. olive oil (or bacon fat), until lightly browned

ADD:
1½ lbs. shrimp, shelled (or use 1 pkg. frozen shrimp, defrosted)
1 jar (5 oz.) chicken, drained of broth

SAUTÉ:
2 minutes, tossing lightly, until shrimp are light pink

ADD:
1½ cup long grain rice
1 tsp. saffron (or use 1 pkg. prepared saffron rice), and toss to coat grains of rice with oil

ADD:
3 cups water
3 chicken bouillon cubes (or 3 tsps. instant bouillon)
3 sprigs parsley (optional), chopped coarsely, and reduce heat

SIMMER:
20 minutes, uncovered, stirring occasionally with a fork until liquid is almost absorbed by rice

ADD:
1 can (8½ oz.) peas, drained
¼ lb. pepperoni (or salami), sliced thin, toss to warm, and serve immediately

Variations:
Add or substitute, as desired, cooked sausages, canned oysters, mussels or clams, drained artichoke hearts or asparagus spears

Serves 4–6

• •

Lobster Fra Diavolo

EASY TO DO: a small amount of lobster goes a long way in this dish, because the sauce is so rich and delicious.

SAUTÉ:	*2 Tbs. chopped onion*
	1 clove garlic, minced
	2 Tbs. chopped parsley, in:
	2 Tbs. olive oil, till onion is wilted
ADD:	*1 can (5 oz.) lobster meat,* and toss lightly
ADD:	*1 can (16 oz.) plum tomatoes,* drained
SIMMER:	5 minutes, covered
FLAMBÉ WITH:	*2–4 Tbs. brandy,* warmed
SERVE ON:	Giant Croutons (p. 173) or boiled rice

Serves 3

• •

Soft-Shell Crabs

EASY TO DO: *if* the crabs have been cleaned. The first time we bought this delicacy, we were about to leave the Maryland fish store when I thought to ask if the crabs had been cleaned. They hadn't. The owner demonstrated the grisly process while gaily shouting to her regular customers, "Here's a couple bought four crabs but don't know how to clean them!"

DREDGE:	*Soft-shell crabs,* cleaned, 1–2 per person, in:
	Crushed Ritz cracker crumbs (or, traditionally, flour, but the salty flavor from the crackers is very good)

SAUTÉ IN: *Butter,* about 2 Tbs. per serving, until crabs
                 are golden on both sides—they cook very fast

ADD: *Fresh lemon juice* to taste, and spoon pan juices
                 over crabs

SERVE WITH: French bread and Asparagus Salad (p. 159)

Serves 1

• •

Shrimp Tempura

MODERATE TIME: this delicious Japanese meal is quickly prepared, but it must be cooked in small batches. Have your diners
ready to queue up and eat.

Can be prepared ahead of time:

BEAT: *2 eggs* with a fork till light and fluffy

ADD: *⅔ cup beer*
                 1 cup flour
                 Dash salt, pepper, and mix thoroughly

ADD: *1½ lbs. shrimp,* peeled (or 1 pkg. frozen
                 shrimp, thawed), and toss to coat each shrimp
                 well

Before serving:

HEAT: *1 pt. vegetable oil* in deep pot until very hot

ADD: Shrimp, cooking a few at a time very quickly,
                 until golden brown

Variations: Repeat Tempura process with a selection of
                 sliced onions, green peppers, eggplant, and
                 sweet potatoes for a complete dinner

Serves 4

• •

Sautéed Shellfish

Easy To Do: fresh shrimp, scallops, or mussels are ideal, but canned or frozen shellfish can be used.

SAUTÉ:	*2 cloves garlic,* minced, in: ¼ *lb. butter,* until lightly browned
ADD:	*1½ lbs. shelled shrimp, scallops, or mussels* *4 Tbs. chopped parsley*
SIMMER:	5–10 minutes, being careful not to overcook
SERVE ON:	Giant Croutons (p. 173) or thick slices of French bread

Serves 4

• •

Sautéed Oysters

Easy To Do: the oysters can be cooked with Worcestershire sauce OR white wine for two completely different—and delicious —meals.

SAUTÉ:	*1 pt. drained oysters,* canned or frozen, in: *4 Tbs. butter,* cooking very fast until done
ADD:	*2 Tbs. chopped parsley* *3 Tbs. Worcestershire sauce OR ¼ cup dry white wine,* and stir until heated
SERVE ON:	Giant Croutons (p. 173) or patty shells

Serves 3

• •

Clams Marinara

Easy To Do: marvelous, but for true clam addicts only.

SAUTÉ: *2 cloves garlic,* minced
                1 small onion, chopped fine, in:
                2 Tbs. olive oil

ADD: *1 can (8 oz.) tomato sauce*
                ½ cup dry white wine
                1 pint canned clams, drained

SIMMER: 5 minutes, uncovered

SERVE WITH: Rice or French bread and chopped parsley for
                garnish

Serves 3

• •

Sautéed Snails

MODERATE TIME: this makes an exquisite, and expensive, supper;
I recommend it only for those who are already in love with escar-
gots, since they are not too attractive to prepare.

SAUTÉ: *2 garlic cloves,* minced
                1 medium onion, minced, in:
                1 stick butter, stirring over high heat until
                golden

ADD: *2 cans (7½ oz. each) snails*—about 3 dozen
                total—and simmer on very low heat 10 min-
                utes

ADD: *¼ cup chopped parsley,* stir and cook about 2
                minutes

SERVE ON: French bread or Giant Croutons (p. 173) to sop
                 up the marvelous sauce

Serves 2 (or 4–6 as an appetizer)

• •

Seafood Risotto

MODERATE TIME: an Italian dish similar to the Spanish Paella;
it is easier to prepare and very good.

SAUTÉ: *1 medium onion,* chopped coarsely
                1 clove garlic, minced, in:
                2 Tbs. olive oil

ADD: *1 cup uncooked rice,* stirring to coat with oil
                3 cups water and 3 chicken bouillon cubes, bring
                   to boil and reduce heat

SIMMER: 15 minutes, uncovered

ADD: *2 cups cooked seafood:* shrimp, clams, crabmeat,
                   mussels or tuna fish

SIMMER: 10 minutes, uncovered

STIR IN: *1 Tb. butter*
                4 Tbs. grated Parmesan cheese
                2 Tbs. parsley (optional), and serve at once

Serves 4

• •

Fillets Amandine

EASY TO DO: even my children, who are not too fond of fish, love it when done this way.

SAUTÉ: *4 large fillets* (sole, flounder, snapper, etc.), in:
                    4 Tbs. butter, until just barely done, turning
                    once—this is very quick, and the flavor of the
                    fish depends on its not being overcooked

ADD: *¼ cup blanched, slivered almonds,* and fry till
                    golden, adding more butter if needed

ADD: *2 Tbs. lemon juice,* swirl and pour sauce over
                    fillets

SERVE WITH: Boiled new potatoes and Artichoke Salad (p.
                    159)

Serves 4

• •

Brook Trout

EASY TO DO: a superlative meal if you've been lucky enough to catch fresh trout, but the frozen ones are also fine.

SAUTÉ: *4 small trout* (2 10-oz. pkgs., thawed), in:
                    2 Tbs. butter, being careful not to overcook

SPRINKLE   *Salt, pepper*
WITH: *Juice 1 lime* (or lemon)

SERVE WITH: German Pan-fried Potatoes (p. 53) and fresh
                    asparagus

Serves 4

• •

Trout Amandine

EASY TO DO: follow directions for Brook Trout, but omit seasonings and juice, pour off fat, and remove trout from pan.

ADD TO PAN: *4 Tbs. butter,* heating till bubbly
               4 ozs. (½ can) blanched, slivered almonds, and
                  shake pan until almonds are lightly browned
ADD: *Juice 1 lemon,* and serve at once

Serves 4

• •

Sherried Tuna Supper Sandwiches

EASY TO DO: a very inexpensive and good dinner; the following
amounts allow two sandwiches per person.

DRAIN: *2 cans (7 oz. each) tuna,* solid pack white meat
                  recommended, and mash with fork
ADD: *Mayonnaise,* just enough to give body to the
                  tuna
               2–4 Tbs. dry sherry, and mix thoroughly
SPREAD ON: *8 slices white bread*
ADD: *8 slices Swiss cheese*
               8 slices white bread
SAUTÉ IN: *2 Tbs. butter,* covered on fairly low heat, until
                  golden on one side
ADD: *2 Tbs. butter,* and turn carefully
SAUTÉ: Covered (so that cheese will melt), until golden
SERVE WITH: Tomato Mushroom Salad (p. 162)

Serves 4

• •

Curried Shrimp

MODERATE TIME: in India, the hotter the weather, the hotter the curry, but I recommend adding this spice judiciously.

Can be prepared ahead of time and reheated:

SAUTÉ:	*2 medium onions,* chopped fine, in:
	3 Tbs. bacon fat (or olive oil), until lightly browned
ADD:	*4 tart apples,* peeled and chopped coarsely, and cook till soft, adding more fat if needed
ADD:	*1 lb. peeled shrimp* (fresh, frozen, or canned), and toss lightly until pink
ADD:	*1½ cups water*
	1 tsp. curry powder (imported preferred), or more to taste, bring to boil and reduce heat
SIMMER:	30 minutes, covered, stirring occasionally and mashing the apples with a spoon
SERVE WITH:	Boiled rice
	Assorted condiments: chopped banana, nuts, hard-boiled eggs, coconut, chutney
Variations:	Substitute 1 lb. cooked meat or poultry for shrimp

Serves 4

• •

Shrimp Fondue

EASY TO DO: this is ready in minutes and is very welcome on a cool evening.

HEAT:	*1 can (10 oz.) undiluted cream of shrimp soup*, over low flame, stirring until hot but not boiling
ADD:	¼ *cup sherry* ½ *tsp. prepared mustard* *4 oz. Swiss cheese*, slivered, and stir until cheese is melted
SERVE WITH:	*French bread*, cubed, speared on a fork or skewer and dipped into Fondue

Serves 3

• •

One-Pot Spaghetti

MODERATE TIME: this is real outdoorsman fare, or as my husband phrases it, "superglop."

SAUTÉ:	*1 medium onion*, chopped fine (or 1 Tb. instant onion) *1 garlic clove*, minced, in: *1 Tb. bacon fat* (or oil)
ADD:	*1 lb. chopped beef*, and brown quickly, breaking up with a fork
ADD:	*1 can (1 lb. 12 oz.) plum tomatoes*, undrained *1 cup red wine* ½ *cup water* *4 ozs. (½ pkg.) thin spaghetti*, broken into small pieces *1 Tb. oregano* *Garlic salt*, pepper to taste *4 slices salami (optional)* cut into thin strips

BOIL: 1 minute, and reduce heat

SIMMER: 25 minutes, covered, stirring occasionally and
                 breaking up tomatoes

Serves 4

• •

Romanoff Casserole

EASY To Do: delicious, nutritious and solicitous of your pocket-
book, this cooks in one pot in fifteen minutes.

SAUTÉ: *1 lb. chopped beef,* in a very hot, deep pot

ADD: *6 cups water,* and bring to boil

ADD: *1 Tb. instant minced onion*
                 1 tsp. garlic salt
                 1 pkg. (8 oz.) noodles, and cook till tender (8–
                    10 minutes)

DRAIN: Water off (or scoop off excess with a spoon)

STIR IN: *1 Tb. Worcestershire sauce*
                 1 Tb. chives (optional)
                 1 pkg. (8 oz.) cottage cheese
                 ½ pt. sour cream, stirring until just hot

SERVE WITH: Tossed green salad

Serves 4

• •

Sausage Wedges

EASY TO DO: an adaptation of the marvelous wedges that we
gobble up at the Danbury (Connecticut) Fair each year.

BROWN:
: *8 pork sausages* (if you like hot spices, use
Italian hot or sweet sausages), pricking to
release fat, until thoroughly cooked

DRAIN:
: On paper towels, and pour off fat in pan

ADD TO PAN:
: *6 Tbs. olive oil*
6 green peppers, sliced thin
1 red pepper (optional), sliced thin
3 onions, sliced thin, and brown on high heat

ADD:
: Cooked sausages, cover and simmer 15–20 minutes, pouring off any excess fat

SERVE ON:
: Italian wedge rolls or Italian bread, sliced
lengthwise

Serves 4

• •

Pizza Supper Sandwiches

EASY TO DO: the "pizza" flavorings are a particular favorite
with the children.

SPRINKLE:
: *4 slices white bread* with:
Olive oil
Oregano
Garlic salt

ADD, MAKING SANDWICHES:	*4 oz. Mozzarella cheese,* sliced thin
	8 slices salami
	4 slices tomato (Beefsteak tomatoes are marvelous if you can get them)
	4 slices white bread
SAUTÉ IN:	*2 Tbs. butter,* covered, over fairly low flame, until lightly browned; turn, add more butter if needed, and cook until cheese is melted.

Serves 4

• •

Welsh Rarebit

EASY TO DO: somehow this is especially welcome when the vacation weather has fallen short of expectations.

MELT:	*1 Tb. butter,* in saucepan
ADD:	*½ cup beer,* and cook over low flame till just hot
STIR IN:	*1 lb. cheddar cheese,* slivered
	1 Tb. Worcestershire sauce
	½ tsp. prepared mustard (optional)
SIMMER:	Until cheese is melted, stirring constantly, and serve immediately; this will be ready very quickly
SERVE ON:	French bread, sliced one-inch thick

Serves 4

• •

German Pan-fried Potatoes

SAUTÉ: *3 onions, sliced thin,* in:
              3 Tbs. bacon fat (or oil), until limp and slightly
                 browned

ADD: *2 cans (16 oz. each) sliced new potatoes,* drained
                 and rinsed

SAUTÉ: Over medium heat, turning often, until browned
                 (add more bacon fat if necessary)

Serves 4–6

• •

Robust Noodles

COOK: *4 ozs. (½ pkg.) noodles* as directed on package,
                 and pour off water

ADD: *1 Tb. butter*
              4 oz. cottage cheese
              4 Tbs. sour cream
              1 Tb. chives, stir until mixed and serve imme-
                 diately

Serves 4

• •

Artichoke Hearts and Peas

MELT: *3 Tbs. butter*

ADD: *1 can (15 oz.) artichoke hearts,* drained and
               rinsed
               1 can (8½ oz.) baby peas, drained
               1 tsp. garlic salt

SIMMER: 5 minutes, or until vegetables are heated

Serves 4

• •

Mushrooms and Sour Cream

SAUTÉ: *1 lb. mushrooms,* chopped coarsely, in:
               4 Tbs. butter, until tender

ADD: *1 Tb. instant minced onion*
               4 Tbs. dry white wine (optional)
               4 Tbs. sour cream, stir until hot but not boiling

Serves 4

• •

Garlic Tomatoes

SAUTÉ: *1 pt. cherry tomatoes* in:
               ⅓ stick butter
               1 tsp. garlic salt, over moderate heat, tossing
               until tomatoes are completely hot

Serves 2–4

• •

Dilled Zucchini

BOIL: *4 medium zucchini,* scrubbed and sliced ¼ inch
               thick, until just "fork-tender"; drain

ADD: *2 Tbs. fresh dill* (or 2 tsp. dried dill)
               4 Tbs. grated Parmesan cheese
               1 Tb. butter (optional), and stir until cheese is
               just slightly melted

Serves 4

• •

Eggplant Parmesan

SLICE: *1 medium eggplant* ½ inch thick (peeled or un-
               peeled, according to your taste)

SAUTÉ IN: *2 Tbs. olive oil* sprinkled with
               1 tsp. garlic salt, cooking over fairly low heat
               until first side is tender; turn

ADD: *4 Tbs. Parmesan cheese* to cooked side, and sauté
               underside until done, adding more oil if neces-
               sary

Serves 4

• •

Peaches with Mincemeat

MELT: 2 Tbs. butter, on low heat

ADD: 1 can (1 lb. 14 oz.) peach halves, drained and
                 filled with:
                 Prepared mincemeat, about 1 spoonful each

COOK: 10 minutes, covered

Variation: Can also be prepared on charcoal grill, omitting
                 butter and wrapping tightly in aluminum foil

SERVE WITH: Pork chops, ham, or poultry

Serves 4

• •

Sautéed Bananas

MELT: 2 Tbs. butter, over low heat

ADD: 4 bananas, peeled and split lengthwise, and cook,
                 turning once, until tender

ADD: Lemon juice (or sugar if serving for dessert)

Serves 4

• •

Additional Menu Suggestions

Besides the recipes given for barbecuing and sandwiches, many of
those suggested for travel dinners can be prepared on the campstove as well; the following are recommended although some will
take longer than those suggested in this chapter.

FROM A LONG DAY'S JOURNEY

Roast Beef and Deviled Egg Supper
Steak Tartare
Mexican Beef
Mushroom and Beef Casserole
Wiener Schnitzel (serve hot)
Tailgate Smorgasbord
Chicken Kiev (serve hot)
Calzone
Italian Wedges
Bread Farci
Shellfish Rémoulade
Crab-stuffed Tomatoes
Curried Shrimp Salad
Chef's Salad

FROM THE SPORTS ARENA

Beef Fondue (with modified sauces)
Boeuf Bourguignon
Hamburger Stroganoff
Hamburger Cassoulet
Chili Con Carne
Slope Soup
Cocido
Goulash Pot
Veal Goulash
Hot Sauce Hot Dogs
Curried Chicken Salad
Tropical Chicken Salad
Chicken Potato Salad
Baby Brook Trout
Caviar Supper Sandwich
Cioppino
Salade Niçoise
Cheese Fondue

3

THE RED GLOW
OF COALS

Can there be someone left who doubts the superlative flavors of a charcoaled steak? Or chicken? Or shish kebab? What about skewered shrimp, basted swordfish steak, marinated pork, grilled lambsteak, bananas in bacon? Whether you build a fire on the beach, set up hibachis at a football game, hang a grill over the side of a boat, or just linger by a campfire roasting marshmallows, the results are almost invariably good.

Since barbecuing is as suited to special outings as to camping out, I've indicated at the beginning of each recipe what part of the preparations can be completed at home. Teriyakis (p. 62), for instance, can be preassembled on skewers, wrapped tightly in foil, and transported in an ice chest. Marinated meats can be packed in tightly closed containers and taken along, gathering flavor as you travel (or they may be prepared on the spot, at least a half hour before grilling). When the camping cook wants to get chores done early, the heading "Can be prepared at home . . ." should be interpreted as also meaning "Can be easily prepared ahead of time on the campgrounds."

Most of the parks and beaches we've visited have made some sort of provisions for cooking out, but a few have required slightly more of a mechanical background than our family possesses. I remember one particularly intricate setup, a grate bolted to cement blocks, with an opening too small to admit a decent-sized piece of wood. Charcoal was the only possibility, but it was a heavily wooded, windy site, and the fire hazard was very real.

To forestall culinary disaster in the more unpredictable situations, it's wise to stash away some newspapers, charcoal, and a sandwich grill. It's also a good idea to have a contingency plan for scrounging up a campstove meal if the fire fails.

Among the following fair-weather suggestions, I've included vegetables, fruits, and desserts that can also be barbecued. As mother and chief chef of the family, I find nothing more appealing than a complete meal, from appetizers to dessert, cooked on the grill by father, the master barbecuer. After all, besides being the cook on a blissful day off, I'm also chief dishwasher, and I don't mind having an occasional pot-less meal, served by firelight.

MENU SUGGESTIONS

(Recipes marked * are included in this book; others are store-bought, standard items.)

Shrimp Wrapped in Bacon*
Steak Teriyaki*
Pineapple Slices Barbecued*
Fried Rice (canned)
Cookies

*

Guacamole Dip*
Mexican Burgers*
Tortillas (canned)
Kidney Bean Salad*
Barbecued Fruits*

*

Marinated Artichoke Hearts
Barbecued Lamb*
Foiled Garlic Bread*
Garbanzo Salad*
Peach Melba*

*

Water Chestnuts Wrapped in Bacon*
Pork Saté*
Herb Bread*
Spinach Salad*
Foiled Plums*

*

Cheese and Crackers
Sweet and Sour Spareribs*
Grilled Eggplant*
Foiled Potatoes*
S'Mores*

*

Charcoaled Appetizers*
Chicken Teriyaki*
Corn on the Cob*
Salad
Sherried Rum Cake*

*

Pickles and Pretzels
Shish Kebab*
Fried Rice (or Skewered Potatoes)
Blueberries with Sour Cream*

*

Low-Cal Dip* with Raw Vegetables
Charcoaled Swordfish Steak*
Asparagus Salad*
Foiled Apples*
—a good diet menu.

• •

Charcoaled Appetizers

EASY TO DO: start the fire early, or cook these at the side of the
grill in time to munch with cocktails.

Can be prepared at home and wrapped in foil:

ASSEMBLE ON   Water chestnuts, wrapped in bacon
SKEWERS ONE   Shrimps, wrapped in bacon, and cherry tomatoes
OR MORE OF   Dates pitted, wrapped in bacon
THE FOLLOWING   Rumaki: lobster chunks and sliced water chest-
COMBINATIONS: nuts, wrapped in bacon
       Cocktail sausages (or cocktail frankfurters) and
       pineapple chunks (or crab apples)

Before serving:

BROIL: 10 minutes or more, until bacon and cocktail
       sausages are lightly browned

• •

Charcoaled Steak

EASY TO DO: everyone has his own favorite way of cooking a
steak, and I give you ours, with two variations to suit the weather
or mood.

Can be prepared at home and wrapped in foil:

RUB: *3 lbs. Sirloin* (or Porterhouse) Steak with:
                  1 tsp. garlic salt
                  Freshly ground pepper
                  1 Tb. dry mustard
                  2 Tbs. Worcestershire sauce. Wrap tightly

Before serving:

BROIL: 5–8 minutes each side, to desired doneness

Variations: Cream ½ stick butter with 2 Tbs. chives OR
                  1 oz. blue cheese and spread on top of cooked
                  steak

SERVE WITH: Foiled Potatoes (p. 87) and salad

Serves 4

•   •

Steak Teriyaki

EASY TO DO: a less expensive cut of steak may be used for this
well-seasoned, quick-cooking meal.

Can be prepared at home and wrapped in foil:

SLICE: *2 lbs. boneless steak,* in thin strips across grain

MARINATE IN: *1 clove garlic,* minced
                  ½ onion, chopped fine
                  1 Tb. powdered ginger (optional)
                  4 Tbs. soy sauce
                  ¼ cup dry white wine

THREAD ON: *Skewers,* and wrap tightly in foil

Before serving:

BROIL: 3–5 minutes on hot coals

SERVE WITH: Chinese Fried Rice (2 cans, punctured and
                  heated at side of fire)

Serves 4

• •

London Broil

MODERATE TIME: a marvelous combination of flavor and textures
that can be varied to suit your taste; it is easier to cook if you
select meats of uniform thickness.

Can be prepared at home and wrapped in foil:

ASSEMBLE: *4 pork sausages*
                  4 chicken livers, wrapped in:
                  4 half-slices of bacon (secure with toothpicks)
                  4 small lamb (or veal) chops seasoned with:
                  Garlic salt, pepper, tarragon or dill
                  1 lb. London Broil Steak (or Club Steak), sea-
                     soned with:
                  Garlic Salt, pepper
                  4 medium tomatoes

Before serving:

CHARCOAL: In the order listed above, allowing about 20
                  minutes for the sausages, 15 minutes for the
                  livers, 5–10 minutes for the chops and steak,
                  5 minutes for the tomatoes

SLICE: Steak into 4 portions

SERVE WITH: Foiled Garlic Bread (p. 175)

Serves 4 (generously!)

• •

Beef Shish Kebab

EASY TO DO: just cut up the meat and vegetables ahead of time and let everyone skewer and cook his favorite concoction.

Can be prepared at home and wrapped in foil:

CUBE: *1½ lbs. boneless steak* (top round, top sirloin, etc.), trimmed of all fat and gristle

MARINATE IN: *½ cup red wine*
                 1 tsp. garlic salt
                 ¼ cup olive oil

ASSEMBLE: *16 cherry tomatoes*
                 4 bananas, quartered
                 8 small onions, peeled
                 8 mushroom caps
                 4 precooked sausages (optional), halved
                 Bacon

Before serving:

THREAD: *Skewers* with meat and vegetables, wrapping some in the bacon, and charcoal to desired doneness

Variations: See page 84 for almost infinite combinations of flavors

Serves 4

•   •

UNITED NATIONS BURGERS

EASY TO DO: from the All-American standby to these international flavors is just a matter of seasoning. I like to serve at least two different "nations" (mix the egg and beef and season half, say, Oriental, and the other half, Mexican). For a big cook-out, it's fun and very dramatic to set up the whole works.

Can be prepared at home and packed in foil

Oriental Burgers

MIX:	*1 egg,* beaten with a fork until fluffy
	1½ lbs. chopped beef
	10 water chestnuts, chopped coarsely
	2 scallions, chopped fine
	¼ cup soy sauce
	Salt, pepper
SHAPE INTO:	4 patties, and charcoal to desired doneness
SERVE WITH:	Soy sauce
	Hamburger buns

Serves 4

• •

Mexican Burgers

MIX:	*1 egg,* beaten with a fork until fluffy
	1½ lbs. chopped beef
	¼ cup chili sauce
	1 Tb. instant minced onion
	Garlic salt
	1 Tb. grated Parmesan cheese
SHAPE INTO:	4 patties, and charcoal to desired doneness

SERVE WITH: Parmesan cheese
               Shredded lettuce
               Tortillas (1 can), heated

Serves 4

• •

French Burgers

MIX: *1 egg,* beaten with a fork until fluffy
               1½ lbs. chopped beef
               1 jar (4½ oz.) mushroom pieces, drained
               2 Tbs. chopped parsley
               Red wine, as much as can be absorbed
               Garlic salt, pepper

SHAPE INTO: 4 patties, and charcoal to desired doneness

SERVE WITH: French bread, cut into thick slices

Serves 4

• •

Greek Burgers

MIX: *1½ lbs. chopped beef*
               4 oz. cottage cheese
               5 sprigs parsley, chopped fine
               2 Tbs. chopped mint
               Salt

SHAPE INTO: 4 patties, and charcoal to desired doneness

SERVE WITH: Syrian flatbread or buns

Serves 4

• •

Italian Burgers

MIX:

1 egg, beaten with a fork until fluffy
1½ lbs. chopped beef
4 Tbs. Mozzarella cheese, chopped fine
4 Tbs. salami, chopped fine
1 Tb. oregano
Garlic salt, pepper to taste

SHAPE INTO: 4 patties, and charcoal to desired doneness

SERVE WITH: Italian rolls

Serves 4

• •

Scandinavian Burgers

MIX:

1½ lbs. chopped beef
½ cup sour cream
2–4 Tbs. blue cheese, crumbled
Garlic salt, pepper

SHAPE INTO: 4 patties, and charcoal to desired doneness

SERVE WITH: Thick slices of black bread or pumpernickel

Serves 4

• •

Canadian Burgers

SHAPE: *1½ lbs. chopped beef* into 4 patties

ADD: *Salt, pepper* to taste
                4 slices blue cheese
                4 slices Canadian bacon, and charcoal in a sand-
                    wich grill, bacon side down last

SERVE WITH: Steak sauce
                Hamburger buns

Serves 4

• •

SAUCES FOR CHARCOALED HAMBURGERS

EASY TO DO: there is an ice-cream parlor near us that lists, among other choices, Hamburger #14—served with Hot Fudge Sauce. I must admit that I haven't tried that one, but I can recommend the following.

Can be prepared at home and packed in thermos bottles or jars

Blue Cheese Sauce

BLEND: *2 Tbs. blue cheese,* crumbled
                3 Tbs. milk
                ½ cup sour cream

SERVE: Hot or cold

• •

Wine Sauce

SAUTÉ: *3 Tbs. chopped scallions* in:
            ½ stick butter

ADD: *¼ cup red wine,* bring to boil and cook 1 minute

• •

Bordelaise Sauce

SAUTÉ: *2 Tbs. instant minced onion* in:
            2 Tbs. butter

ADD: *½ cup red wine*
            ½ cup beef bouillon, and boil 10 minutes

STIR IN: *1 tsp. lemon juice* (or 1 Tb. currant jelly)

• •

GARNISHED HAMBURGERS

EASY TO DO: I don't know how to gild a lily, but there are many ways to dress up a charcoaled hamburger. Select a combination of the following chopped vegetables, cheeses, meats, seasonings, and sauces, and set them up as condiments.

Can be prepared at home and packed in jars and foil:

SHAPE: *1½ lbs. chopped beef* into 4 patties

VEGETABLES: Chopped radishes, pickles, onions, mushrooms (raw or cooked), green pepper, sliced avocado, tomatoes, grilled eggplant

CHEESES: Sliced Swiss, cheddar, Provolone, Mozzarella; blue cheese, Ricotta

MEATS: Cooked sausages or chicken livers, crumbled bacon, sliced ham, Canadian bacon, salami, liver paté

SEASONINGS: Russian Dressing, Tabasco, sour cream, mustard-mayonnaise, soy sauce

SPICES: Oregano, mint, parsley, chili powder, ginger— and salt and pepper

Serves 4

• •

Barbecued Lamb

EASY TO DO: *if* the butcher will bone a leg of lamb for you; otherwise allow extra time to cut a steak off this beast. The meat should be handled as if it were Sirloin, and it will taste just as good, if not better.

Can be prepared at home and wrapped tightly:

MARINATE: *3 lbs. leg of lamb, boned, in:*
                1 garlic clove, minced
                2 Tbs. olive oil
                ½ cup red wine
                1 tsp. each salt, pepper, basil, thyme (or marjoram)

Before serving:

CHARCOAL: Lambsteak in a sandwich grill, closing it tightly to flatten steak, and baste with marinade; cook about 8 minutes on each side, until medium rare (don't overcook—it should be almost as rare as Sirloin)

SERVE WITH: Foiled Garlic Bread (p. 175) and salad

Serves 4

• •

Center Cut Lambsteaks

EASY TO DO: this cut of meat is comparatively new on the supermarket scene. It is very good and inexpensive when it can be found.

Can be prepared at home and wrapped tightly:

MARINATE: *4 lambsteaks* (about ½ lb. each), cut across leg, in:
                   6 Tbs. red wine
                   1 garlic clove, minced
                   1 Tb. rosemary (or mint)

Before serving:

CHARCOAL: 3 minutes each side, basting with marinade; lambsteaks should be served very pink on the inside

SERVE WITH: Foiled Potatoes (p. 87)

Serves 4

• •

Barbecued Lamb Chops

EASY TO DO: be careful not to overcook these delicacies.

Can be prepared at home and wrapped tightly:

MARINATE: *4 thick loin lamb chops,* in:
                 2 Tbs. olive oil
                 2 Tbs. red wine
                 2 garlic cloves, minced

Variations: Substitute soy sauce, or lemon juice and mint,
                 for the wine and garlic

Before serving:

CHARCOAL: To desired doneness, basting occasionally

SERVE WITH: Corn on the Cob (p. 86) and Grilled Eggplant
                 (p. 86)

Serves 4

• •

Lamb Shish Kebab

EASY TO DO: allow each person to skewer a selection from the
following, or select other vegetables and fruits suggested on
page 84.

Can be prepared at home and wrapped in foil:

CUBE: *2 lbs. boneless lamb,* trimmed well

MARINATE IN: *Juice 1 lemon*
                 ½ cup red wine
                 1 clove garlic, minced
                 ¼ cup olive oil
                 Salt, pepper, tarragon (or mint)

ASSEMBLE: *1 small eggplant,* cut in ¾-inch cubes
                   2 medium apples, cored and quartered
                   1 can (8¼ oz.) pineapple chunks
                   8 small onions, peeled
                   2 green peppers, cut into eighths
                   Bacon

Before serving:

THREAD: *Skewers* with meat and vegetables, wrapping
                   some in the bacon, and charcoal to desired
                   doneness

Serves 4

• •

Grilled Lamb Patties

EASY TO DO: very inexpensive, with excellent flavor.

Can be prepared at home and wrapped in foil:

MIX: *1½ lbs. ground lamb*
                   ½ cup chopped pine nuts (or peanuts)
                   ½ cup chopped raisins
                   ¼ cup chopped parsley
                   ¼ cup chopped onion
                   2 eggs, beaten with a fork until fluffy
                   1 cup bread crumbs
                   Salt, pepper, nutmeg (optional)

SHAPE INTO: 4 patties

Before serving:

CHARCOAL: To desired doneness

SERVE WITH: Sourdough bread and Onion-Tomato Salad (p.
                   162)

Serves 4

• •

Breast of Lamb

MODERATE TIME: lamb ribs are not quite as good as spareribs, but at a third of the price they're very tasty!

Can be prepared at home and wrapped tightly:

MARINATE: *3 lbs. breast of lamb* in:
                            2 Tbs. Worcestershire sauce (or 4 Tbs. soy sauce)
                            4 Tbs. olive oil
                            Juice 1 lime (or lemon)
                            ½ cup white wine

Before serving:

CHARCOAL: 30–45 minutes, basting occasionally with marinade

SERVE WITH: Herb Bread (p. 176) and grilled tomatoes

Serves 4

• •

Barbecued Veal Chops

EASY TO DO: these should be basted frequently and they will be juicy and flavorful.

CHARCOAL: *4 thick veal chops,* over low fire

BASTE WITH: *½ stick melted butter,* mixed with:
                            Juice 1 lemon
                            4 Tbs. white wine

Variation: Baste with equal parts soy sauce and olive oil

Serves 4

• •

Barbecued Ham Steak

Easy To Do: Use the marinade or the variation for a succulent meal.

Can be prepared at home and packed in jar:

MIX: 2 tsps. dry mustard
                2 Tbs. brown sugar
                ¼ cup sherry

Before serving:

BASTE: 2 lbs. center cut ham steak (precooked) with sherry mixture, and charcoal to desired doneness

Variation: Substitute olive oil and soy sauce for the sherry

Serves 4

• •

Barbecued Pork Chops

Easy To Do: allow plenty of time for the pork to cook thoroughly and to absorb the charcoal flavor.

Can be prepared at home and packed tightly:

MARINATE: 4 thick center-cut pork chops in:
                ½ cup ketchup
                4 Tbs. vinegar
                2 Tbs. olive oil
                2 Tbs. brown sugar

Before serving:

CHARCOAL: Pork chops, on low fire until thoroughly cooked
                 (about 30 minutes, depending on the thickness
                 of the chops)—baste frequently

SERVE WITH: Spinach Salad (p. 165) and Foiled Rye Bread
                 (p. 176)

Serves 4

• •

Pork Paté

ELABORATE: this cooks fairly quickly but takes time to prepare.
However, every minute is well spent because of the superb
flavor and low cost of this really special dinner.

Can be prepared at home and packed tightly:

MARINATE: *2 lbs. boneless pork,* cut into 1-inch cubes and
                 trimmed of all fat, in:
                 1 clove garlic, minced
                 1 small onion, chopped fine
                 Juice 1 lemon
                 4 Tbs. soy sauce
                 1 Tb. brown sugar (or white sugar)
                 3 Tbs. peanut butter

Before serving:

ASSEMBLE: Meat on skewers (don't pack too tightly)

CHARCOAL: 15–20 minutes, until thoroughly cooked but not
                 dry

SERVE WITH: Chinese Fried Rice (2 cans) and salad

Serves 4

• •

Sweet and Sour Spareribs

ELABORATE: after experimenting with at least a dozen marinades, we've found this combination outstanding.

Can be prepared at home and packed tightly:

MARINATE: *3½ lbs. pork spareribs* in:
                4 Tbs. vinegar
                4 Tbs. soy sauce
                6 Tbs. white wine (or sherry)
                1 garlic clove, minced
                1 Tb. instant minced onion
                1 Tb. brown sugar

Before serving:

MIX: *1 Tb. cornstarch* in:
                1 Tb. water, and heat in small pan at side of grill

ADD: Marinade, stirring until hot and clear

CHARCOAL: Spareribs on slow fire, basting frequently with sauce, until thoroughly cooked (about 1 hour)

Serves 4

• •

FRANKFURTER TREATS

EASY TO DO: use any of the following ideas to embellish hot dogs for a quick, inexpensive, and good dinner.

Can be prepared at home and packed tightly:

Marinated Hot Dogs

MARINATE: *8 frankfurters* in:
                 1 cup French dressing (p. 189 or bottled)
                 ¼ cup dry wine (optional)

• •

or

Stuffed Frankfurters

SPLIT: *8 frankfurters,* lengthwise
FILL WITH: *2 cups poultry stuffing* (½ pkg.), prepared ac-
                 cording to directions on package
WRAP IN: *8 slices bacon,* securing with toothpicks
                 Any extra stuffing may be wrapped in foil and
                 cooked on the grill

• •

or

Skewered Franks

ASSEMBLE: *8 frankfurters,* cut crosswise in 4 chunks each
                 8 small bananas (or pineapple chunks) cut in
                 4 chunks each, on:
                 8 skewers

Before serving:

CHARCOAL: Frankfurter Treats until done

Variations: Serve charcoaled frankfurters with bottled Béar-
                   naise Sauce

Serves 4

• •

Grilled Cornish Hens

MODERATE TIME: a scrumptious way to cook these fine birds.

Can be prepared at home and packed tightly:

SPLIT: *2 Cornish hens* (thawed) halfway through the
                   underside of the back bone until they can be
                   spread open for cooking

MARINATE IN: *½ cup red wine*
                   2–4 Tbs. Worcestershire sauce
                   1 tsp. each garlic salt, pepper

Before serving:

CHARCOAL: 15–20 minutes, each side, basting with marinade
                   (allow less time if cooking in a sandwich
                   grill)

SERVE WITH: German Potato Salad (p. 167) and Foiled Plums
                   (p. 89)

Serves 2–4

• •

Chicken Teriyaki

MODERATE TIME: barbecued chicken is especially good with Japanese seasoning.

Can be prepared at home and wrapped tightly:

MARINATE: *1 frying chicken, cut up, in:*
½ cup soy sauce
¼ cup white wine
1 clove garlic, minced
1 tsp. powdered ginger

Before serving:

CHARCOAL: 15 minutes, each side, basting occasionally
Variation: Add ¼ cup ketchup and 2 Tbs. vegetable oil to above marinade
SERVE WITH: Chinese Fried Rice (2 cans) and Peaches with Mincemeat (p. 56)

Serves 4

• •

Foiled Chicken Dinner

EASY TO DO: serve each person his own meal-in-a-packet.

Can be prepared at home and wrapped in foil:

ALLOW PER *½ large chicken breast*
PERSON: *2 carrots, pared and sliced lengthwise*
1 potato, peeled and sliced lengthwise
1 small onion (optional), sliced thin
Salt, pepper, seasonings to taste (vary them!)
Large pat of butter

WRAP IN: *Aluminum foil,* dull side out, in the above order

Before serving:

BROIL: 30–40 minutes, wrapped, until chicken is done
                and potatoes are tender

• •

Charcoaled Swordfish Steak

EASY TO DO: even my fish-hating friend loves fresh swordfish
when it is barbecued with this sauce.

MIX: *½ stick melted butter*
                Juice of 1 lime
                2 Tbs. Worcestershire sauce (optional)
                Garlic salt, pepper

CHARCOAL: *2 lbs. swordfish steak* (1–1½ inch thick) on hot
                coals, baste frequently with butter sauce, and
                cook about 8 minutes each side (don't over-
                cook—fish is done when there is no translu-
                cence and the flesh is firm in center)

Variation: Substitute lemon juice and soy sauce for the lime
                and Worcestershire

SERVE WITH: Shoestring potatoes (1 can) and salad

Serves 4–6

• •

Grilled Trout

EASY TO DO: fresh fish is superb, but frozen trout may also be used most successfully.

CHARCOAL: *4 trout* (2 pkgs. frozen trout, thawed) directly on grill

BASTE WITH: *Melted butter* (about ½ stick)
                 Juice of ½ lemon, cooking about 5 minutes each side, and turning carefully with a spatula

SERVE WITH: Remaining melted butter, if desired

Serves 4

• •

Shellfish in the Shell

EASY TO DO: There couldn't be a simpler or better way of cooking king crab or lobster tails.

CHARCOAL: *1 lb. thawed shellfish* (frozen lobster tails or king crab legs) directly on grill

BASTE WITH: *Melted butter* (about ½ stick)
                 Garlic salt, wherever the shells are cracked open, for about 15 minutes, turning occasionally

SERVE WITH: Remaining melted butter
                 Lemon wedges

Serves 2–3

• •

Barbecued Shrimp

EASY To Do: the first time I served this, my daughter said it was so good that even people who hated shrimp would like it.

Can be prepared at home and packed in foil:

MARINATE: 1½ *lbs. peeled shrimp in:*
              4 Tbs. soy sauce
              2 Tbs. olive oil
              Dash garlic salt, ginger (optional)

ASSEMBLE: Shrimp on skewers and wrap in foil

Before serving:

CHARCOAL: 2–4 minutes each side, depending on size of shrimp—be careful not to overcook

Variation: Substitute 4 Tbs. white wine, juice 1 lemon and 2 Tbs. chopped parsley for the soy sauce

Serves 4

• •

Charcoaled Scallops

EASY To Do: shrimp and other shellfish may also be cooked in this manner; for a grand feast use a variety of skewered fish.

Can be prepared at home and wrapped in foil:

MARINATE: 1½ *lbs. bay scallops* (or large scallops, halved) in:
              4 Tbs. ketchup
              4 Tbs. vinegar
              4 Tbs. soy sauce
              1 Tb. brown sugar

ASSEMBLE: Scallops on skewers, with:
                   16 cherry tomatoes
                   2 green peppers, cut in small slices—wrap in
                        foil

Before serving:

CHARCOAL: 5 minutes, or until just done, being careful not
                        to overcook, and basting with marinade if
                        desired

SERVE WITH: Grilled Eggplant (p. 86) or Onion Rings (p.
                        88)

Serves 4

• •

Shish Kebabs

EASY TO DO: besides the traditional lamb shish kebab, there are
many other ingredients that lend themselves to skewer cookery
for an almost endless succession of feasts. Marinate a selection
of meat and/or fish (almost a half pound per person), prepare a
variety of complementary fruits and vegetables, and watch the
diners go to town assembling their skewers! My husband warns
that since the eye is often larger than the fire, one shouldn't pack
the skewers too full; one should, however, be ready for seconds
(and thirds, and fourths . . .).

Can be prepared at home and packed in foil and jars:

MARINATE: *Cubed meat*—beef, lamb, pork, liver, sausages—
                        in:
                   ½ *cup red wine,* ¼ *cup olive oil, seasonings* to
                        taste

MARINATE: *Cubed or shelled fish*—oysters, crabmeat, lob-
               ster, shrimp, scallops, swordfish, fillets—*in:*
               ¼ cup olive oil, 4 Tbs. soy sauce or lemon juice,
               1 Tb. sugar (optional), seasonings to taste

PREPARE: *Vegetables*—tomatoes, cherry tomatoes, onions,
               mushroom caps, green pepper, zucchini,
               eggplant, water chestnuts, artichoke hearts,
               olives, canned new potatoes, sweet potatoes—
               washing, paring, and cubing them as needed

PREPARE: *Fruits*—canned pineapple chunks, apples,
               spiced crab apples, bananas, grapes, cumquats
               —washing, paring, and cubing them as
               needed

CUT: *Bacon slices* in thirds, to use for wrapping
               around other ingredients as desired for flavor,
               juiciness, and "skewer stability" (e.g. pine-
               apple chunks often fall apart without bacon)

Before serving:

THREAD: Skewers, and charcoal to desire doneness

Variations: A few great, if unlikely, combinations to whet
               your imagination are oysters and liver
               wrapped in bacon with mushroom caps and
               crab apple; beef and lobster cubes with toma-
               toes, onions, and banana; pork and shrimp in
               a soy marinade with green peppers, water
               chestnuts, and pineapple

● ●

CHARCOALED VEGETABLES

To round out the main course, many vegetables and fruits can be
barbecued on an outdoor grill, either directly on the fire or

wrapped in aluminum foil. When using foil, however, it is important to remember to wrap foods with the dull side out, since the shiny side reflects heat and prevents thorough cooking.

Corn on the Cob

SOAK: *8 ears of corn,* with silk removed but husks intact, in water 20 minutes

CHARCOAL: 30–40 minutes on top of grill (or less if directly in fire)—turn occasionally

Serves 4

• •

Grilled Eggplant

SLICE: *1 large eggplant* into ½-inch-thick slices

BASTE WITH: *½ cup olive oil* (or butter, or bacon fat)
                 Garlic salt, pepper

CHARCOAL: 15 minutes or until tender, turn and baste occasionally

Serves 4

• •

Foiled Potatoes

SCRUB: *4 large baking potatoes,* and cut a one-inch divot
             in the center of each

ADD: *Butter*
             Garlic salt, pepper, to the cavity, replace divot
             and wrap potato in aluminum foil

CHARCOAL: 1 hour at side of grill or edge of coals

Serves 4

• •

Potato-Onion Packet

SLICE: *2 cans (16 oz. each) new potatoes,* drained and
             rinsed, ¼ inch thick
             1–2 large onions, ⅛ inch thick

ADD: *Butter*
             Salt, pepper, oregano (optional), and wrap in
             foil

CHARCOAL: 20 minutes or until potatoes are hot

Serves 4

• •

Grilled Onion Rings

SLICE: *2 Bermuda onions,* peeled, about ⅓ inch thick
CHARCOAL: 5 minutes, basting with:
                  Butter

Serves 4

• •

BARBECUED FRUITS

Easy To Do: place fruits at the edge of the grill, charcoal until
just hot and tender, and serve as a side dish or dessert.

BASTE: *Apples,* 1–2 per serving, sliced ½ inch thick,
                      with:
                  Butter
                  Lemon juice (preferably fresh)
BASTE: *Bananas,*   per serving, split lengthwise, with:
                  Butter
                  Brown sugar
BASTE: *Pineapple slices,* 1–2 per serving, with:
                  Butter
                  Soy sauce for main course; *sugar* for dessert

• •

Foiled Plums

SPLIT: *8 red plums,* remove pits and wrap in aluminum
                  foil

CHARCOAL: 10–20 minutes, or until hot, tender, and juicy

Serves 4

•   •

Foiled Apples

CORE: *4 large, tart apples,* fill with:
                  Butter
                  Cinnamon (or nutmeg), and wrap in aluminum
                  foil

CHARCOAL: ½ hour or until tender

Serves 4

•   •

4

A LONG DAY'S
JOURNEY

A neighbor phoned the other day, with some desperation in her voice, to ask when the cookbook would be ready. "We just drove home from Maine," she said, "and it took us an hour to get a hamburger and a cup of coffee." It's because of this sort of experience that I have tried to find a varied collection of recipes for food to be consumed while driving from here to there.

Whether you plan to eat in the car or to make a quick stop at a picnic area, you can save both time and money taking your meals along with you. There is also the added advantage of being able to eat *what* you want *when* you want it. Too often we have searched in vain for a suitable restaurant at an appropriate hour, driving on far longer than our stomachs or moods could bear. And now the "limited access" highways make it even harder to find a decent meal without the risk of finding yourself lost in a maze of underpasses.

Besides these practical considerations, part of the fun of a mobile life is thinking up new surprises and taste treats to munch en route. Somehow the time seems to pass faster, and the children seem to stay quieter, with a variety of snacks and the anticipation of a good meal.

There are all sorts of ways to make a lunch or dinner more pleasing than a piece of cheese between two slices of bread. Interesting combinations of ingredients and spreads can enliven a sandwich luncheon (see Chapter VI). Or better yet, set up a smorgasbörd at a picnic rest area or serve a cold roast chicken for a grand (and quite inexpensive) supper.

If you are planning to picnic, most states now recognize that people do get hungry, and have set up some very pleasant roadside picnic areas. These are free, equipped with tables and (hopefully) good shade trees. If you have time for longer stops or for slight detours, investigate the State and National Parks that you will find listed on most road maps. There are many more scattered about the country than you might believe, and a lot of them not only allow picnicking, but have swimming, hiking, "scenic vistas," and space enough to unwind after a long drive.

The recipes for journeying, then, range from the fairly simple to the elaborate. Most of the meals can be served in the car, but some really need the accoutrements of a picnic table. Handing your husband a stuffed tomato while he's negotiating a turnpike can be catastrophic, while Wiener Schnitzel, the pride of some very fine chefs, can be handled amazingly well en route.

By using various devices to pack foods that aren't usually picnic fare, travel meals can become epicurean. An aluminum foil baking dish can hold an Armenian pie or pirozhki; large jars can store fruit compote or shrimp salad; plastic bags can house hors d'oeuvres, and baby-food jars can carry the dips.

Snacks, the more the merrier, are especially welcome on a long drive, and can be planned to complement a meal. Cucumber slices, celery, and cherry tomatoes make a delicious finger salad; cooked eggplant sticks, raw cauliflower, and carrots are good vegetable hors d'oeuvres. Fruit, cheese, raisins, and nuts are all high in protein and vitamins and they are always in demand.

To supply drinks during a journey, a large jug of lemony iced tea is most refreshing at any season. For the children, choose juices and sodas with screw-cap tops, since a half-full can of Coke can get to be a nuisance after many miles.

Other hints for car cuisine:

Avoid sticky desserts and even potato chips (too greasy)—judge
a food by that sensible M & M slogan, and make sure it "melts
in the mouth, not in the hand."

Carry in the glove compartment a small, fairly blunt knife, and
a bottle opener.

Use as many disposable items as possible—paper plates, cups
for cold and hot liquids, plastic utensils, and many napkins.

Save aluminum trays and pieplates from frozen foods for trans-
porting foods.

Whenever possible, pack things in the order in which they will
be used, with hors d'oeuvres on top and desserts on the bottom.

If serving canned foods, such as a paté or French Fried Onion
Rings, open the cans at home, leaving an inch unsevered so
the lid will stay on until serving time.

When serving pieces of chicken, a boned breast is much easier
to handle—especially for the driver.

Plan on preparing double portions of elaborate recipes, leaving
the first at home in the freezer: two meals for the work of one.

MENU   SUGGESTIONS

(Recipes marked * are included in this book; others are store-
bought, standard items.)

In transit:

Pickle Rolls*
London Broil Dinner*
Cherry Tomatoes and Raw Peas
Brownies*

*

Smoked Salmon Hors d'oeuvres*
Wiener Schnitzel*
Eggplant Sticks*
Pumpernickel with Sweet Butter
Pecan Cake*

*

Cold Cut Roll Ups*
Pirozhki*
Raw Vegetables
Butterscotch Squares*

*

Smoked Bacon Rinds
Italian Wedges*
Fresh Fruit
Bourbon Balls*

*

For picnics:

Pretzels and Nuts
Tailgate Smorgasbörd*
Chocolate Whiffs*

*

Guacamole Dip* and Crackers
Steak Tartare*
Buttered Pumpernickel
Marinated Mushrooms*
Strawberry Shortbread*

*

Raw Mushrooms and Cauliflower
Cocktail Sauce*
Chive "Fried" Chicken*
Garbanzo Salad*
Instant Strawberry Shortcake*

*

Deviled Eggs*
Crab-stuffed Tomatoes*
Banana Bread*
Cinnamon Shortbread*

● ●

*

London Broil Dinner

MODERATE TIME: you can prepare this the day of the trip, or
buy a larger steak to serve hot for dinner the night before—two
meals for the work of one.

BROIL:	*1 lb. London Broil steak* (or other high quality, thick boneless steak) seasoned with:
	Garlic salt, pepper
	Dash Worcestershire sauce (or more to taste) to desired doneness
SLICE:	Steak paper-thin, across grain, and chill if prepared ahead
MIX:	½ *stick butter,* at room temperature
	2 Tbs. chopped parsley
	2 Tbs. chopped scallions
SPREAD ON:	*4 soft buns,* and fill with the sliced steak

Serves 4

● ●

London Broil Variations

MODERATE TIME: prepare as for London Broil Dinner, but substitute either of the following spreads for the parsley-butter.

MIX: *½ stick butter,* at room temperature
                            4 Tbs. chopped chives
                            Dash Worcestershire sauce

MIX: *1 tsp. each horseradish and dill weed*
                            4 Tbs. sour cream

• •

Marinated Beef Salad

EASY TO DO: save roast beef from Sunday dinner, or buy it unsliced from a delicatessen for this main dish salad.

SLICE: *1–1½ lbs. cooked rolled roast beef* (top sirloin,
                            eye round, etc.), into thin strips

MARINATE IN: *2 Tbs. olive oil,* mixed with:
                            6 Tbs. vinegar
                            1 medium onion, sliced paper thin
                            1 clove garlic, minced
                            1 Tb. capers
                            2 tomatoes (optional), sliced thin

SERVE WITH: Avocado Soup (p. 169) and French bread

Serves 4

• •

Roast Beef and Deviled Egg Supper

EASY TO DO: buy the roast beef slices at the delicatessen, or save money and serve a rolled roast to the family a few days before the journey.

ROLL:	*8–12 slices roast beef* around:
	8–12 sticks of Swiss cheese (8 oz. pkg. unsliced cheese cut into "fingers") and secure with toothpicks
SLICE:	*4 hard-boiled eggs* lengthwise, and remove yolks
MIX:	Egg yolks, mashed with a fork, with
	3 Tbs. mayonnaise
	1 tsp. prepared mustard
	1 tsp. anchovy paste (optional), and fill egg whites
PACK IN:	Plastic containers or paper plates covered with aluminum foil
SERVE WITH:	Buttered Party Rye and dill pickles

Serves 4

• •

Steak Tartare

EASY TO DO: there are strong opinions about this dish—I adore it, but my husband abhors it; so check your audience beforehand, or serve it as part of a smorgasbörd.

COMBINE: *2 lbs. chopped round* (or other top quality beef)
               2 Tbs. minced red onion
               2 Tbs. chopped parsley
               1 tsp. capers
               ½ inch anchovy paste
               1 Tb. thick steak sauce (bottled)
               3 raw egg yolks (optional)—mix lightly and
                   chill until ready to serve

SERVE WITH: *Buttered pumpernickel bread* (or rye bread)
               Garlic salt, pepper
               Steak sauce

Serves 4–6

• •

Armenian Meat Pie

MODERATE TIME: the unusual flavors in this recipe are enhanced
when the pie is served at room temperature.

PREPARE: *1 pie crust* (1 stick) following package direc-
                   tions

MIX: *1½ lbs. chopped beef*
               1 egg, beaten with a fork
               1 onion, minced
               ½ cup milk
               2 tsps. nutmeg
               4 tsps. cinnamon
               ¼ cup chopped pine nuts (or 4 Tbs. chopped
                   parsley) and spoon into pie crust

BAKE: 25 minutes at 400°, and cut into wedges

SERVE WITH: Marinated Green Beans (p. 162)

Serves 4

• •

Cold Meatloaf With Cheese

MODERATE TIME: Roquefort or Blue Cheese makes the dish rise above its modest origins—and modest price.

MIX: *2 eggs,* beaten with a fork
                2 lbs. ground beef
                1 clove garlic, minced
                1 Tb. instant minced onion
                1 cup milk
                1 pkg. (4 oz.) Roquefort (or blue cheese)
                Garlic salt, pepper to taste

SHAPE: Into loaf, and place in aluminum foil pan or
                baking dish

SPRINKLE   *Bread crumbs*
WITH:

BAKE: 45 minutes, at 350°, drain off fat and refrigerate

SERVE: In thick slices, with more cheese if desired, and
                French Bread

Serves 6–8

• •

Mexican Beef

MODERATE TIME: this meal-in-a-thermos is equally good for a skating or skiing outing, or campstove cookery.

SAUTÉ: *2 onions,* chopped coarsely
                2 green peppers, seeded and chopped, in:
                2 Tbs. olive oil, until slightly browned

ADD: *2 lbs. chopped beef,* and brown quickly

ADD: *1 cup raisins*
                ½ cup black olives, sliced
                2 cups beef bouillon (or 1 cup water plus 1
                bouillon cube) and bring to boil

ADD: *1 cup Minute Rice,* and stir thoroughly

SIMMER: 10 minutes, covered, and pack in wide-mouth
                thermos bottle

Serves 6–8

• •

Mushroom and Beef Casserole

EASY TO DO: the "casserole" is a wide-mouth thermos bottle,
and the meal is perfect for an autumnal drive.

BROWN: *1 lb. ground beef*
                2 Tbs. instant minced onion in:
                1 Tb. olive oil

ADD: *1 can (8 oz.) mushroom pieces,* drained
                1 tsp. garlic salt
                ½ cup red wine
                2 cups water—stir on high heat, till boiling

ADD: *6 oz. (½ pkg.) noodles*—cook uncovered 8 min-
                utes, stirring occasionally

SPOON OFF: As much water as possible

ADD: *2 Tbs. butter*
                2 Tbs. Worcestershire sauce
                2 Tbs. Steak sauce—stir and pack in half-gallon
                thermos bottle

SERVE IN: Hot-cups, and don't forget to bring along spoons

Serves 4

• •

Wiener Schnitzel

MODERATE TIME: the price of veal may scare you at first, but remember, there is no waste. The cutlets feed four nicely and make a feast when served with a chilled bottle of dry white wine.

POUND:	*4 large veal scallopine,* to 1/4 inch thickness
DREDGE IN:	*1/2 cup flour,* then dredge in
	1 egg and 1 Tb. water, beaten with a fork; then dredge in
	1/2 cup bread crumbs
SAUTÉ IN:	*Vegetable oil,* 1/4 inch deep and very hot, till golden brown on both sides; total time should be 3–5 minutes
DRAIN ON:	Paper towels, wrap in foil and chill
SERVE WITH:	Sliced lemon and capers, soft buttered rolls and Cucumber Dill Salad (p. 160)

Serves 4

• •

Tailgate Smorgasbörd

EASY TO DO: this is fun for everyone, since the cook does not have to cook, and the children can eat whatever they desire. Pack up the different items in plastic bags or foil, and arrange them on a paper platter at the picnic table.

SPREAD:	*4 slices salami* with
	1 pkg. (4 oz.) blue cheese, roll and secure with toothpick

CUBE:	¼ *lb. Swiss cheese* (unsliced)
	¼ *lb. bologna* or roast beef (unsliced), and thread on toothpicks
SPREAD:	*8 slices "party pumpernickel" bread* with
	1 pkg. (3 oz.) cream cheese and top with
	4 slices Nova Scotia salmon, cut in half
SERVE WITH:	*Cherry tomatoes*
	Dill pickles
	Breadsticks
	Egg rolls or Shrimp rolls (precooked from delicatessen)
	1 jar. (8 oz.) pickled herring

Serves 4

• •

Chilled Roast Chicken

EASY TO DO: preparation is close to nothing, but allow enough time to roast and chill this delicious bird.

PREPARE:	*4 lbs. roasting chicken* by removing gizzards and excess fat (saving liver for paté if desired)
PUT IN CAVITY:	*Garlic salt, terragon*
ROAST:	1 hour at 350°, basting occasionally with
	¼ *stick butter,* melted
ROAST:	¼ hour more at 400°, or until skin is nicely browned
CHILL:	1 hour or more, and remember to pack along a carving knife
SERVE WITH:	Onion-Tomato Salad (p. 162) and buttered buns

Serves 4

• •

Chicken Kiev

ELABORATE: a really special treat for everyone (but the cook), this was the basis of my husband's birthday dinner on the boat, as well as the start of some fine car trips.

POUND:	*2 chicken breasts,* boned, split and skinned, until very flat (I use wax paper and a huge mallet)
SEASON WITH:	*Garlic salt, pepper*
ADD:	*4 tsp. butter,* cut lengthwise into sticks *4 tsp. chopped chives,* and fold chicken to form a sealed pouch
DREDGE IN:	*Flour,* about ¼ cup, then dredge in: *1 egg,* beaten with a fork and 1 Tb. water, then in: *½ cup bread crumbs,* resealing pouches if needed
DEEP-FRY IN:	*8 oz. vegetable oil,* very hot, until golden brown
DRAIN:	On paper towels and serve hot or chilled
SERVE WITH:	French Fried Onion Rings (1 can) and Cucumber Dill Salad (p. 160), and for a birthday gathering, add Avocado Soup (p. 169) and Champagne Punch (p. 193)

• •

Herb-Broiled Chicken

EASY TO DO: dieters will be especially appreciative of this highly seasoned chicken, since there are no calories added in the cooking.

PREHEAT OVEN: 425°

SEASON: *2 split chicken breasts* (large) with:
                2 Tbs. marjoram or thyme
                Garlic salt, pepper to taste. Place in aluminum
                    foil broiler pan, skin side down

BAKE: 15 minutes and then turn oven to "broil"

BROIL: 5 minutes on each side, until lightly browned

COOL: On paper towels, and serve at room temperature
                    or chilled

SERVE WITH: Garlic bread sticks (store-bought) and Cole
                    Slaw (p. 161)

Serves 4

• •

Chive "Fried" Chicken

MODERATE TIME: this fried chicken is actually baked—eliminat-
ing pots, fats, and spatterings—and tastes like a Southern specialty.

PREHEAT OVEN: 350°

SPLIT: *2 large chicken breasts,* removing excess fat

DIP IN: *5⅓ oz. evaporated milk* (in paper plate)

MIX: *1 cup cornflake crumbs* (or breadcrumbs)
                6 Tbs. dried chives
                1 tsp. garlic salt, pepper

DREDGE: Chicken breasts in mixture and place skin side
                    up in aluminum foil dish

BAKE: 1 hour without turning or basting; wrap and
                    chill

SERVE WITH: German Potato Salad (p. 167) and cherry toma-
                toes

Serves 4

• •

Beef Pirozhki

MODERATE TIME: a Russian tea room wouldn't approve of this
recipe, but it simplifies a marvelous dish and makes it packable
for the car.

SAUTÉ: *1 lb. ground beef* on high heat until browned
                (draining off fat carefully)—remove from
                heat

ADD: *1 Tb. instant minced onion*
                1 Tb. each nutmeg and cinnamon
                ½ cup red wine (or beef bouillon)

UNROLL: *1 pkg. refrigerator Crescent Dinner Rolls* (8),
                and pat out into thin triangles (if not avail-
                able, roll out refrigerator biscuits)

ADD: Meat mixture, fold into pouches, and place on
                greased aluminum foil pan

BAKE: 15 minutes, at 400°

SERVE WITH: Mushroom Pirozhki (see below) for a grand
                feast

Serves 2 as is or 4 with Mushroom Pirozhki

• •

Mushroom Pirozhki

SAUTÉ: *1 onion, chopped fine,* in:
              3 Tbs. butter, until golden

ADD: *½ lb. mushrooms,* chopped coarsely
              1 cup raisins (optional), and cook 5 minutes on
              low heat

ADD: *4 Tbs. sour cream,* and proceed as in Beef Pi-
              rozhki

• •

Calzone

ELABORATE: though not authentic this still takes patience. Be
sure to have an extra supply of napkins with you.

UNROLL: *2 pkgs. Crescent Dinner Rolls* (16), and pat
              out into very thin triangles

FILL WITH: *4 ozs. Mozzarella cheese,* slivered
              3 ozs. Prosciutto or salami, slivered—seal and
              moisten edges to form an envelope

DEEP-FRY IN: *1 pt. vegetable oil,* a few at a time, till golden

DRAIN ON: Paper towels; wrap in aluminum foil and pack
              in insulated container

SERVE WITH: Assorted raw vegetables and pickles

Serves 4

• •

Italian Wedges

Easy To Do: whether you call them wedges, submarines, grinders, or heroes, these are guaranteed to make a hit with the man of the house—or the car, as the case may be.

SPLIT:	*4 large Italian rolls* (or "hard rolls")
SPRINKLE	*1 onion,* minced
INSIDES WITH:	*½ green pepper,* chopped fine
	2 Tbs. oregano
	Garlic salt, pepper
	Olive oil, enough to coat rolls without making them soggy
ADD:	*4 slices salami* (one for each roll)
	4 slices bologna, ham or prosciutto (one for each roll)
	4 slices Provolone cheese (one for each roll)
	8 slices tomato, cut very thin (two for each roll)
	8 slices dill pickle, cut lengthwise very thin (two for each roll)
SERVE WITH:	Chianti, of course!

Serves 4

• •

Bread Farci

Easy To Do: the name does not imply a farcical creation, just the French term to indicate that the bread is stuffed with goodies.

PREPARE: *1 large loaf French bread* for stuffing, by slic-
                ing lengthwise, opening flat, scraping out
                crumbs to leave the loaf ½ inch thick

SPREAD WITH: *½ stick butter,* at room temperature
                1 tsp. garlic salt
                2 Tbs. chopped chives

ADD: *4 slices salami,* slivered
                4 slices bologna, slivered
                ¼ lb. Swiss or Mozzarella cheese, slivered
                2 Tbs. chopped onion
                2 tomatoes, sliced
                4 anchovy fillets (optional)

SLICE: Loaf crosswise into 2-inch-thick pieces, reassem-
                ble, and wrap tightly with aluminum foil

Serves 4

• •

Shellfish Rémoulade

EASY TO DO: the flavors meld to produce a refreshing hot weather
treat.

THAW: *1 pkg. (8 oz.) cooked crab meat* or shrimp
                (peeled)

MIX WITH: *1 cup mayonnaise*
                *1 Tb. each tarragon, parsley, prepared mustard,
                capers*
                1 garlic clove, chopped fine
                2 sweet pickles, chopped fine

SERVE ON: *Bed of Iceberg lettuce,* with breadsticks and
                cherry tomatoes

Serves 4

• •

Crab-stuffed Tomatoes

EASY TO DO: this has the virtue of being both high in flavor and low in calories.

HOLLOW: *4 large tomatoes,* reserving pulp and turning upside down to drain

MIX: *1 pkg. (8 oz.) frozen cooked crab meat,* thawed
               2 Tbs. finely chopped onion
               2 scallions, finely chopped
               ½ cucumber, finely chopped
               Garlic salt, pepper, capers to taste
               Juice 2 limes
               Small amount of mayonnaise, just enough to bind salad
               Tomato pulp, chopped

FILL: Tomatoes with crab meat mixture and wrap each in foil

SERVE WITH: French Fried Onion Rings (canned) and Shoestring Potatoes (canned)

Serves 4

• •

Curried Shrimp Salad

EASY TO DO: the unusual ingredients in this salad go equally well with tuna fish for a much less expensive meal.

RINSE: *3 cans (4½ oz. each) shrimp* in fresh water, and drain

MIX WITH: *¾ cup mayonnaise*
                      2 tsps. curry powder (or more to taste)
                      ½ lb. seedless grapes

FILL: *8–12 frankfurter rolls* with mixture, wrap in
                      foil and pack in insulated carrier

Serves 4–6

• •

Chef's Salad

EASY TO DO: there are so many variations of this recipe that I suggest letting your imagination run wild with extra fillips.

MIX: *1 small head Iceberg lettuce,* torn in pieces
                      1 small head Boston or romaine lettuce, torn
                      2 tomatoes, cut into chunks
                      1 cucumber, diced
                      4 scallions, chopped fine
                      ¼ lb. cold cuts (ham, bologna or salami), slivered
                      ¼ lb. Swiss cheese or Munster, slivered

TOSS WITH: *French dressing,* p. 189

SERVE WITH: Buttered pumpernickel bread

Serves 4

• •

5

THE
SPORTS ARENA

A special outing should be an event. I'm not suggesting going quite as far as the group of spectators we observed at a Yale–Harvard game: they unfolded a picnic table, spread it with linen (yes, linen), brought out a pair of candlesticks, and, in perfect center, positioned a large bowl of fruit. However, on closer inspection, the fruit proved to be plastic. I'm for the real thing.

Oysters on the half shell. Champagne, well chilled in an insulated cooler. Cold Roast Cornish Hen, or a chafing dish fondue. Expensive and too much work? We share the cost and the cooking chores for a Grand Occasion.

At the other end of the tailgate arena are the sporting events in which we are the participants—skiing, sailing, hiking, swimming, etc. For these, one wants dishes that are fairly simple to prepare but highly nutritious and filling. Chilled seafood or chicken salads are delights by the seashore, while a hearty soup and a hunk of cheese is a welcome pick-me-up for a cold skier—and "pick-me-up" is unfortunately close to a description of my style on the slopes.

MENU SUGGESTIONS

(Recipes marked * are included in this book; others are store-bought, standard items.)

A Football Feast

Oysters on the Half Shell
Cocktail Sauce*
Cold Roast Cornish Hen*
Ratatouille*
Nut Bread*
Champagne

*

Winter Sports

Mixed Nuts
Hamburger Cassoulet*
Fruit and Cheese Dessert*
Irish Coffee* and Cinnamon Cocoa*

*

A Breezy Sail

Steak Tartare in Mushroom Caps*
Cioppino*
French Bread
Brownies*
Chablis

*

A Summer Outing

New Potato Appetizer*
Shrimp Salad in Avocado Boats*
Banana Bread*
Meringue Kisses*
Champagne Punch*

*

A Football Spread

Southern Shrimp*
Beef Fondue*
Raw Vegetable Sticks
Bourbon Balls*
Sangria*

*

Skiing or Skating

Toothpick Skewers*
Cheese Fondue*
Italian Bread
Fruit
White Wine

*

A Spring Picnic for Two

Caviar and Toast
with
Chopped Egg Whites and Yolks, Minced Onion
Baby Brook Trout* on Lettuce Bed
Buttered Pumpernickel
Strawberries in Wine*
Riesling

*

By the Seashore

Avocado Soup*
Salade Niçoise*
Rolls
Strawberry Shortbread*
Wine Spritzer*

Beef Wellington

ELABORATE: fifteen minutes preparation amidst one hour's baking time completes this fantastic dish—my husband didn't believe it, so I timed it—and it is good served hot or cold for a sensational tailgate buffet.

ROAST: *2½ lbs. eye round roast* for 40 minutes at 300° (other good quality beef may be used, but the roast should not be more than 4 inches in diameter)

While meat roasts:

ROLL OUT: *1 pkg. buttermilk biscuits* (or pie crust) into a large oval, and spread with:
1 can (2½ oz.) liver paté

TRIM: Beef of all fat and strings and encase in dough

BAKE: 20 minutes more, at 450°, or until crust is lightly brown

SERVE: Hot or chilled, in thick slices

Variation: Duxelles, a cooked mixture of mushrooms, onion, and butter may be substituted for the liver paté

Serves 6

• •

BEEF FONDUE

EASY TO DO: this is one of my favorite meals of all times, and would be spectacular for a football game. It's expensive, because everyone eats to the groaning point, but easy, because each person cooks the meat himself, and then dips it into a variety of sauces.

Can be prepared at home and packed in foil and jars:

CUT: *4 lbs. boneless steak* (London Broil, Sirloin, or other tender cut) into 1 inch cubes, trimmed of all fat

PACK: *Fondue set with forks or bamboo skewers*
              Cooking fuel (sterno or rubbing alcohol, depending on the type of set)
              1 pt. vegetable oil

PREPARE: The following sauces, and/or Sauce Béarnaise (bottled), Sauce Verte (p. 153), Steak Sauce (bottled)

Serves 6

• •

Horseradish Sauce

WHIP: *1 cup low calorie whipped topping* (or 1 cup unwhipped sour cream)

ADD: *2 tsps. prepared horseradish,* or to taste

• •

Soy Sauce Dip

HEAT: *½ cup soy sauce* until bubbling

ADD: *2 Tbs. cornstarch,* dissolved in:
              6 Tbs. water

STIR: Until thickened (this happens very fast; the
                 mixture will have dark spots as sauce cooks,
                 but these will disappear when thickened)

                              • •

Rémoulade Sauce

MIX: *1 cup mayonnaise*
                 ¼ cup dill pickles, chopped fine
                 1 Tb. capers, drained
                 1 hard-boiled egg, chopped fine
                 ½ tsp. prepared mustard
                 1 Tb. each: parsley, chervil, and tarragon

Curry Mayonnaise

MIX: *1 cup mayonnaise*
                 2 tsps. curry powder (or more to taste—it
                 should be quite hot)

Before serving:

HEAT: *Vegetable oil* (1 pt.) until very hot—about 10
                 minutes—and have each person cook his meat
                 to desired degree of doneness.

Serves 6–8

                              • •

Boeuf Bourguignon

MODERATE TIME: this hearty dish is grand for cool weather activities, such as skiing, sailing or skating, and can also be made at a campsite.

Can be prepared ahead of time and reheated:

SLICE:	*2 lbs. boneless steak* (top round is fine) into small, thin pieces
SAUTÉ IN:	*2 Tbs. bacon fat* (or oil), browning quickly
ADD:	*3 cloves garlic,* minced
	1 can (1 lb.) onions, drained and rinsed
	1 can (8 oz.) baby carrots (optional), drained
	1 Tb. flour
	1 tsp. each salt, pepper, marjoram, thyme
ADD:	*1½ cups dry red wine,* stirring until flour dissolves
	1 can (8 oz.) mushrooms, drained
	1 can (1 lb.) new potatoes, drained and rinsed
SIMMER:	½ hour, tightly covered
SERVE WITH:	French bread

Serves 6

• •

Hamburger Stroganoff

EASY TO DO: this quickie is very tasty and filling on a cool day.

Can be prepared ahead of time and reheated:

SAUTÉ: *1 lb. chopped beef*
1 Tb. instant minced onion in:
1 Tb. butter, browning quickly

ADD: *2 cans (10½ oz. each) chicken-noodle soup,* undiluted
1 can (8 oz.) mushrooms, drained
Garlic salt, pepper to taste

SIMMER: 5 minutes, uncovered

ADD: *1 cup sour cream,* stirring until heated but not boiling

Serves 4 for dinner, 6 for lunch

• •

Lasagne

MODERATE TIME: although Lasagne may seem an unlikely choice for the tailgate, it works equally well for a fall picnic or football game; be sure to take along plates, forks, and serving implements.

COOK: *8 oz. lasagne,* following package directions

SAUTÉ: *½ lb. chopped beef* in:
1 tsp. garlic salt, cooking quickly until browned

ADD: *3 cups (1½ jars) prepared spaghetti sauce* (the kind containing meat or mushrooms is best)

LAYER: Aluminum foil pan (8 x 10 inches) with:
Meat Sauce
Lasagne
1 lb. Ricotta cheese (or cottage cheese)
8 oz. Mozzarella cheese, slivered
½ cup grated Parmesan cheese, ending with a thin layer of meat sauce and Parmesan

BAKE: 45 minutes at 325°

SERVE WITH: Spinach Salad (p. 165) or Ratatouille (p. 163)

Serves 8

• •

Hamburger Cassoulet

MODERATE TIME: a very hearty adaptation, this makes a fine
cold weather dinner for six people, or a warming lunch for eight.

Can be prepared ahead of time and reheated:

SAUTÉ: *½ lb. pork sausages* in a deep pot; remove to
                     paper plate and pour off all but 1 Tb. fat

ADD: *1 lb. chopped beef* (or leftover duck or turkey
                     if you're lucky enough to have it) and brown

ADD: *2 cans (16 oz. each) kidney beans,* drained and
                     rinsed
                     Garlic salt, pepper, marjoram, to taste
                     2 cups dry red wine
                     Sausages, cut into 1-inch chunks

SIMMER: ½ hour, covered, adding more wine if sauce be-
                     comes dry

Serves 6–8

• •

Chili Con Carne

Easy To Do: a fast and filling meal almost any time, anywhere.

Can be prepared ahead of time and reheated:

SAUTÉ: 1 lb. chopped beef
2 cloves garlic, minced, in:
1 Tb. olive oil

ADD: 1 onion, chopped fine
1 green pepper, chopped coarsely
1 can (1 lb.) red kidney beans, crushed with a spoon
1 can (6 oz.) tomato paste
2 Tbs. chili powder
1 tsp. oregano
½ tsp. each dry mustard, curry
3 Tbs. wine vinegar

SIMMER: 15 minutes, covered

SERVE WITH: Beer or wine—to cool the taste buds!

Serves 4

• •

Hot Meat balls

Easy To Do: this is a fine luncheon entrée when served in rolls or a grand appetizer for a large group at a football game. It is best when made at least one day ahead of time and refrigerated. Skim off fat before reheating.

Can be prepared ahead of time and reheated:

SHAPE: 1 lb. chopped beef (chuck or round) into about 30 small balls

HEAT:	1 bottle (14 oz.) chili sauce
	7 ozs. (½ bottle) ketchup
	1 tsp. Worcestershire sauce (or more to taste)
	4 Tbs. currant jelly, and stir until jelly is dissolved
ADD:	Meatballs, stirring in gently
SIMMER:	30 minutes, covered
SERVE WITH:	Italian rolls or toothpicks

Serves 4–6 for lunch, 8–10 for an appetizer

• •

Beef Empanadas

MODERATE TIME: similar to turnovers and pirozhki, these are Mexican in origin, and make a marvelous luncheon for a special outing.

Prepare at home and pack in foil:

SAUTÉ:	2 onions, chopped fine, in:
	2 Tbs. olive oil, until lightly browned
ADD:	1 lb. chopped beef, and brown quickly
ADD:	½ cup raisins
	10 black olives, chopped fine
	1 tsp. each salt, pepper
	Sherry, to taste (optional), and simmer 10 minutes
FLATTEN:	16 Crescent Dinner Rolls (or refrigerator biscuits) into thin triangles, fill with beef mixture, fold into pouches and place on aluminum foil pan
BAKE:	15–20 minutes at 400°

Serves 6–8

• •

Goulash Pot

EASY TO DO: preparation time is very short; however, it should should simmer for at least an hour.

Can be prepared ahead of time and reheated:

SAUTÉ:	*1 lb. chopped beef* *1 medium onion,* chopped fine, in: *1 Tb. bacon fat* (or oil)
ADD:	*1 can (1 lb. 12 oz.) plum tomatoes* *2 cups water* *2 cups red wine* (or water) *2 Tbs. garlic salt* *½ lb. sausages,* sliced *1 can (1 lb.) sliced new potatoes,* drained and rinsed
SIMMER:	1 hour, covered
SERVE WITH:	French bread or rolls to sop up the sauce

Serves 8

• •

Wally's Glop

MODERATE TIME: a skiing favorite with children and adults alike. The amounts of meat and cheese may be varied slightly for a richer or leaner dish.

Can be prepared ahead of time and reheated carefully:

SAUTÉ:	*6 slices bacon,* chopped, until partially cooked
	    and add:
	2 medium onions, chopped, cook 3 minutes, and
	    add:
	¾–1 lb. chopped beef, stirring until browned

MIX: Bacon-onion-beef mixture with
                8 ozs. cooked macaroni, drained
                ⅓–½ lb. packaged cheese, diced, in oven-proof
                    dish, reserving some of the cheese to sprinkle
                    on top

BAKE: ½ hour at 350°, or until dish is bubbling, and
                    pour into large, wide-mouth thermos bottle

Serves 6

• •

Moussaka

ELABORATE: there are countless versions of this dish from the
Near East, and this is a comparatively simple one, but it still
takes some time to prepare. The recipe can be easily doubled
for a mob, and would be a marvelous main course for a fall
tailgate spread.

Can be prepared ahead of time and reheated:

SLICE: *2 medium eggplants,* unpeeled, ½ inch thick

SAUTÉ IN: *Vegetable oil,* a few pieces at a time, till lightly
                    browned; set aside on a paper plate

ADD: *2 Tbs. butter*
                2 medium onions, chopped coarsely, and cook
                    till wilted

ADD: *2 lbs. chopped beef*
                1 tsp. each garlic salt, nutmeg, and brown
                    quickly

ADD: *1 jar (14 oz.) spaghetti sauce*
                4 sprigs parsley, chopped
                Dash red wine (optional), and simmer 2 min-
                    utes

LAYER: Eggplant slices and meat mixture in a large, greased casserole or aluminum foil baking pan

BEAT: *4 eggs,* till fluffy

ADD AND BEAT: *1 lb. cottage cheese,* and pour over eggplant and meat mixture

BAKE: 1 hour at 400°, covered till last 10 minutes (increase the time by about 20 minutes if doubling the recipe)

Serves 8

• •

Slope Soup

EASY TO DO: this is especially good for skiers, since it can be made up the night before for an early start to the mountains.

Can be prepared ahead of time and reheated:

SAUTÉ: *1–2 lbs. sausage meat,* in large pot, until browned

ADD: *2 cans (1 lb. each) kidney beans,* drained
                 2 cans (1 lb. each) whole tomatoes, undrained
                 2 onions, chopped fine
                 1 potato, chopped fine
                 Garlic salt, pepper to taste

SIMMER: 1 hour, stirring from bottom occasionally

SERVE IN: "Hot cups"

Serves 8

• •

Cocido

MODERATE TIME: the marvelous taste of this hearty dish makes it particularly suitable for an autumnal luncheon or dinner.

Can be prepared ahead of time and reheated:

SAUTÉ: *1 pkg. (1 lb.) pork sausages* until browned on all sides, and pour off fat

ADD: *1 lb. chopped beef*
                1 garlic clove, minced, browning garlic and beef quickly

ADD: *1 can (1 lb. 12 oz.) tomatoes,* drained slightly
                1 can (1 lb.) chick peas, drained and rinsed
                1 can (14 oz.) string beans (or green peas), drained
                Red wine (optional) to taste—I like to add as much as can be absorbed without making the dish soupy

SIMMER: 20 minutes, covered

SERVE WITH: French bread

Serves 4–6 for dinner, 8 for lunch

• •

Cocido Variations

In Spain, a pot of Cocido makes use of whatever vegetables are on hand; add cooked leftovers or canned potatoes, sweet potatoes, squash, pumpkin, apples, or cabbage.

• •

Vitello Tonnato

EASY TO DO: this is a very fast and completely unauthentic version of the famous Italian cold dish.

Prepare ahead of time:

SAUTÉ:	*6 veal scallopine* (about 1½ lbs.), pounded thin, in:
	Olive oil, just enough to cover pan
	Garlic salt, cooking quickly on high heat until done; drain on towels and let cool
MIX:	*1 can (7 oz.) tuna fish,* mashed with a fork
	Juice 1 lemon
	3 inches anchovy paste
	Mayonnaise, enough to form a thick paste
SPREAD ON:	The scallopine, roll and wrap in aluminum foil (if the scallopine are too thick to roll, top with a lettuce leaf to cover tuna mixture in transit). and chill
SERVE WITH:	*Capers* or chopped parsley, and Italian bread

Serves 6

• •

Veal Goulash

MODERATE TIME: an inexpensive and heart-warming dish.

Can be prepared ahead of time and reheated carefully:

SAUTÉ:	*3 onions,* sliced thin, in:
	2 Tbs. bacon fat (or oil), till limp; push to one side of pan

ADD: *2 lbs. boneless veal,* trimmed and cut in small
                cubes, and brown lightly (with more fat if
                needed)

ADD: *2 tsps. paprika*
                1 cup dry white wine (or beef bouillon)
                1 jar (4½ oz.) button mushrooms, drained

SIMMER: 30–45 minutes, covered, until meat is tender

ADD: *½ cup sour cream,* and stir till hot but not
                boiling; pack in wide-mouth thermos bottle

SERVE WITH: Buttered rolls and Kidney Bean Salad (p. 167)

Serves 6

• •

Hot Sauce Hot Dogs

EASY TO DO: a good, warming dish to serve after skiing or
skating.

Can be prepared ahead of time and reheated:

MIX: *1 Tb. instant minced onion*
                1 Tb. Worcestershire sauce
                2 Tbs. vinegar
                ¼ cup chili sauce
                ½ cup ketchup
                ¾ cup water, and bring to boil

ADD: *12 frankfurters,* quartered

SIMMER: 20 minutes

PACK IN: Wide-necked thermos bottle

SERVE ON: Italian rolls, split

Serves 6

• •

Cold Roast Cornish Hen

MODERATE TIME: baking and basting occasionally are the only
things involved in this inexpensive delicacy; we've found that
half a hen serves one person admirably, but you may want to
provide whole birds for a grand feast.

Prepare ahead of time:

CLEAN: *2 Cornish hens* (about 1½ lbs. each), removing
                 gizzards and excess fat, and sprinkle cavity
                 with:
                 Garlic salt

BAKE: 50 minutes at 350°, basting occasionally with:
                 Butter, and pan drippings

ADD: *Currant jelly (optional),* spooning it over top of
                 birds—this makes a dramatic glaze, but it's a
                 bit sticky to eat with the fingers

BAKE: 20 minutes more at 400°, or until crisply
                 browned, chill and cut in half

SERVE WITH: Eggplant sticks (p. 163) and Cold Rice Salad
                 (p. 168)

Serves 2–4

• •

Chicken Liver Pirozhki

MODERATE TIME: this recipe makes eight rich pirozhki, or turnovers, enough for four people if accompanied by deviled eggs or
a large hors d'oeuvres platter.

Prepare at home and wrap in foil:

SAUTÉ: *4–6 chicken livers* in:
                    4 Tbs. butter, over moderate flame until done.
                    Remove from heat

ADD: *3 oz. cream cheese,* at room temperature, and
                    mash cheese and livers with a fork

ADD: *1 tsp. nutmeg*
                    Brandy, stirring in enough to moisten mixture

FLATTEN: *8 Crescent Dinner Rolls* (or refrigerator bis-
                    cuits) into thin triangles, fill with liver mix-
                    ture, fold into pouches and place on aluminum
                    foil pan

BAKE: 20 minutes at 400°

Serves 2–4

• •

Poultry Turnovers

MODERATE TIME: a good complement to above pirozhki.

MIX: *1½ cups cooked chicken* or turkey, chopped fine
                    1 Tb. each chives, parsley, instant minced onion
                    ½ cup leftover gravy or ¼ cup sour cream

FILL: *8 Crescent Dinner Rolls,* and proceed as above
                    in Chicken Liver Pirozhki

• •

Curried Chicken Salad

EASY TO DO: a light and lovely summer lunch, quickly prepared at home or campsite.

Can be prepared at home and packed in jars:

MIX:
2 cups diced, cooked chicken
½ lb. seedless grapes, halved if large
½ cup mayonnaise
Curry powder to taste—we use lots, but start with a light hand

SERVE WITH: Lettuce leaves and buttered rolls

Serves 4

• •

Tropical Chicken Salad

EASY TO DO: a very refreshing lunch, or a nice supper if served with a hearty appetizer or soup and dessert.

Can be prepared at home and packed in jars:

MIX:
2 cups diced, cooked chicken
½ cup mayonnaise (or half mayonnaise, half sour cream)
1 can (8¼ oz.) pineapple, drained
10 water chestnuts, chopped coarsely
Shredded coconut (optional)

Variation: Substitute canned "Tropical" fruits and bottled
                      blue cheese dressing for the pineapple and
                      mayonnaise

Serves 4

• •

Chicken Potato Salad

EASY TO DO: this is as quick to prepare while you are camping
as it is at home.

Can be prepared at home and packed in jars:

MIX: *2 cups diced, cooked chicken*
              1 can (16 oz.) sliced new potatoes, drained and
                  rinsed
              2 Tbs. vinegar
              ½ cup minced celery
              1 small onion, chopped fine
              1 can (8½ oz.) baby peas (optional), drained
              ¾ cup mayonnaise
              Salt, pepper to taste

Variation: Substitute raw cauliflower, broken into small
                      pieces, for the peas

Serves 4

• •

Baby Brook Trout

EASY TO DO: an extremely simple, absolutely beautiful, and expensive luncheon. I picture it in a quiet grove, with a bubbling brook nearby, enjoyed by two.

CHILL: *1 can Icelandic baby brook trout* (available in gourmet food stores)

MIX: *½ cup mayonnaise*
                  2 Tbs. dry mustard (or more to taste—the sauce should be quite tangy)

PLACE ON: *Boston lettuce leaves,* with sauce poured over the trout

SERVE WITH: Pumpernickel bread, spread with sweet butter, and a chilled Riesling wine

Serves 2

• •

Caviar Supper Sandwiches

EASY TO DO: I include these surprisingly inexpensive sandwiches in this chapter because they are so rich and good that they are best saved for special occasions.

Can be prepared at home and packed in insulated container:

MIX: *4 hard-boiled eggs,* mashed with a fork
                  6 Tbs. finely chopped onion
                  4 Tbs. sour cream (or mayonnaise)
                  2 Tbs. butter, at room temperature
                  4–6 Tbs. salmon (red) caviar

Before serving:

FILL: *12 slices pumpernickel bread,* making 6 sand-
                            wiches

SERVE WITH: Gazpacho (p. 170) and a *light* dessert

Serves 6

• •

Cioppino

MODERATE TIME: a vastly simplified version of the Italian main
course soup.

Can be prepared at home and packed in a thermos bottle:

SAUTÉ: *3 onions,* chopped fine
                         1 green pepper, chopped fine, in:
                         4 Tbs. olive oil, until browned, and reduce heat

ADD: *1 pkg. (8 oz.) shrimp,* thawed, tossing to coat
                            with oil
                         1 can (1 lb. 12 oz.) tomatoes, drained
                         1 can (8 oz.) tomato sauce
                         1½ cups white wine
                         4 sprigs parsley, chopped
                         1 tsp. each garlic salt, pepper, oregano
                         1 can (7 oz.) tuna, drained and broken into
                            small pieces

SIMMER: 10 minutes, crushing tomatoes

SERVE WITH: Italian bread

Serves 4 (6 for lunch)

• •

Shrimp Salad in Avocado Boats

EASY To Do: a delightfully cooling dish on a hot summer's day.

SLICE:	*2 ripe avocados* in half lengthwise, remove pit, and score the flesh down to the skin so that it can be opened up
SPRINKLE WITH:	*Lemon juice,* fresh or bottled, to prevent discoloration
MIX:	*1 pkg. (8 oz.) f.ozen cooked shrimp (peeled),* thawed *4–6 Tbs. mayonnaise* *1 Tb. Worcestershire sauce* *Dash lemon*
PACK:	In insulated container and fill avocados with Shrimp Salad just before serving
SERVE WITH:	French bread and a dry white wine

Serves 4

• •

Salade Niçoise

EASY To Do: boil the eggs, assemble the ingredients and you're set!

Can be prepared at home and packed in jars:

MIX:	*4 hard-boiled eggs,* quartered *1 pt. cherry tomatoes* *1 can (16 oz.) sliced new potatoes,* drained and rinsed *1 large, red onion,* sliced thin

1 can (8¼ oz.) green beans, drained
1 can (13 oz.) tuna fish, drained
8 anchovy fillets
12 black olives
¼ cup olive oil
3 Tbs. vinegar
Garlic salt, pepper to taste

SERVE ON: Lettuce leaves

Serves 6–8

• •

Stuffed Green Peppers

MODERATE TIME: this makes an unusual and inexpensive lunch or light supper.

Can be prepared at home and wrapped in foil:

PREPARE: 1 pkg. (6 oz.) Long Grain and Wild Rice Mix, according to package directions

ADD: 1 can (13 oz.) tuna fish, drained and broken into small pieces
1 Tb. olive oil
Garlic salt, pepper to taste

SIMMER: 6 large green peppers, cored and seeded, in boiling water 3 minutes; drain and fill with rice mixture

SERVE: Hot or chilled, with Nut Bread (p. 173) or sliced French bread

Serves 6

• •

Rice Salad Supper

Easy To Do: a quick and good summer supper.

Can be prepared at home and packed in insulated container:

MIX:	*2 cups cooked rice*
	6 Tbs. olive oil (or more to taste)
	2 Tbs. vinegar (or more to taste)
	1 Tb. each chopped parsley, capers, onion
	Garlic salt, pepper
	1 can (13 oz.) tuna fish, drained
	1 can (8½ oz.) baby peas, drained, or artichoke hearts
CHILL:	1 hour, or more
Variation:	Substitute cubed salami and Swiss cheese for the tuna fish
SERVE WITH:	Lettuce leaves, or fill tomato shells with mixture

Serves 4

● ●

Corn Chowder

Easy To Do: a warming and filling lunch for skating or skiing.

Can be prepared ahead of time and reheated carefully:

SAUTÉ:	*1 lb. bacon,* chopped
	½ cup chopped onions
	½ cup chopped green pepper (optional) until bacon is browned

ADD: *1 can (16 oz.) creamed corn*
                       1 cup (½ can) sliced new potatoes
                       8 oz. packaged cheese, diced
                       1 can (5⅓ oz.) evaporated milk, and stir until
                           cheese begins to melt

ADD: *2 medium tomatoes,* chopped coarsely, and stir
                           until tomatoes are hot and cheese is melted

Serves 6

• •

Cheese Fondue

EASY TO DO: unbeatable on a crisp fall day, and worth every bit
of the effort of packing a fondue set. This is also a big hit with
children and simple to do in a pot on a campstove.

Can be prepared ahead of time and packed in plastic bags:

CUT: *2 lbs. Swiss cheese* into slivers (domestic cheese
                           is fine for this, but not processed cheese)

SPRINKLE   *Flour,* tossing cheese until lightly coated and
WITH: discarding any excess flour

PACK: Cheese mixture, in plastic bag
                       1½ cup dry white wine (in jar)
                       Fondue set, with forks or skewers
                       2 loaves French bread, cut into 1-inch cubes

Before serving:

HEAT: Wine until bubbling (and alert your diners be-
                           cause the Fondue will be ready quickly)

ADD: Cheese mixture, stirring until melted (add a
                           little more wine if mixture becomes too thick)

TO SERVE: Each person spears a chunk of bread to dip and
               swirl in the Fondue. Alpine tradition decrees
               that anyone who drops his bread must pay a
               penalty of a round of drinks or a round of
               kisses—I'll leave the choice to you.

Serves 6–8

• •

6

THE ENLIGHTENED
SANDWICH

Like the "hamburger with a college education," the lowly sandwich can surmount its humble origins and become a gastronomic
delight. Not, perhaps, a filet mignon—though we even had that
while we were skiing one New Year's Day—but a Caviar Sandwich (page 146) will do quite nicely, James, and costs about a
quarter.

Sandwiches are, of course, appropriate for every kind of tailgate meal, and by combining unusual flavors and ingredients, the
variety is limitless. Sandwich casings need not be limited to
bread, but can include hamburger and hot-dog buns, butter rolls,
tortillas and biscuits; different seasonings can be added to butters
and spreads to produce new flavors.

Many of the recipes in this chapter are substantial enough to
qualify as travel dinners, and can supplement the suggestions
given in Chapter 4. They'll make a more nutritional main course,
though, if they're coupled with vegetable sticks, snacks, or a dessert, or if the amount of filling is increased to make a really thick
—and filling—sandwich.

In addition to the following ideas, most of the seafood and
chicken salad recipes in other sections of this book are also excellent to use for sandwiches. Whatever recipe you select, however,
I recommend a lesson learned from the Scandinavian smorgas-

börd: a thin spreading of butter, dressing or cream cheese (or a bed of lettuce leaves for dieters) on both pieces of bread will help to keep the dough fresh and tasty.

Easy To Do
Family Favorite Sandwich

SLICE:	*1 loaf Italian bread,* crosswise, ½ inch thick
SPREAD WITH:	*Butter,* at room temperature *Garlic salt*
ADD:	*4–8 slices roast beef* *2 tomatoes,* sliced very thin *1 onion,* sliced paper-thin *2 dill pickles,* sliced lengthwise very thin *4 slices Swiss* (or Muenster) cheese

Makes 4 sandwiches

• •

Spiced Beef Sandwich

MIX:	*¼ cup mayonnaise* *2 Tbs. steak sauce* *1 Tb. chopped onion* *1 Tb. capers (optional)*
SPREAD ON:	*8 slices rye* (or pumpernickel)
ADD:	*4–8 slices roast beef* *Lettuce leaves*

Makes 4 sandwiches

• •

Dieter's Dream Sandwich

MIX: *4 oz. cottage cheese*
                1 Tb. blue cheese, crumbled
                1 Tb. chopped onion

SPREAD ON: *4 slices diet bread* (or thin-sliced pumpernickel)

TOP WITH: *4–8 slices roast beef,* and wrap individually

Variation: Substitute chili sauce or steak sauce for blue cheese

Makes 4 open-faced sandwiches (about 150 calories each)

• •

Creamy Beef Sandwich

MIX: *4 oz. sour cream*
                1 Tb. dehydrated onion soup mix (or more to taste)
                1 Tb. chives

SPREAD ON: *Hamburger buns*

ADD: *4–8 slices roast beef* (or packaged corned beef)

Makes 4 sandwiches

• •

Rye-Beef Sandwich

SPREAD: *8 slices rye bread* with:
               Russian dressing (bottled)

ADD: *4 sliced pickles* (dill or sweet)
               4–8 slices roast beef

Variation: Substitute butter and French Fried Onion Rings
               (canned) for dressing and pickles

Makes 4 sandwiches

• •

Deviled Ham Sandwich

MIX: *1 can (4½ oz.) deviled ham*
               2 Tbs. mayonnaise
               1 Tb. chopped onion

SPREAD ON: *4 slices white bread*

ADD: *1 avocado,* sliced
               4 slices white bread

Makes 4 sandwiches

• •

Ham Chutney Sandwich

SPREAD: *8 slices whole wheat bread* with:
               Chutney, thin layer on each

ADD: *2 tart apples,* pared and sliced thinly
                4–8 slices boiled ham

Makes 4 sandwiches

• •

Ham and Rye Sandwich

MIX: *½ stick butter,* at room temperature
                1 tsp. dry mustard
                1 tsp. Worcestershire sauce
                2 Tbs. grated Parmesan cheese

SPREAD ON: *8 slices rye bread*

ADD: *4–8 slices boiled ham*

Makes 4 sandwiches

• •

Canadian Club Sandwich

MIX: *½ cup mayonnaise*
                1 tsp. dry mustard

SPREAD ON: *12 slices white bread* (preferably thin-sliced)

COVER 1ST   *4 slices Swiss cheese*
LAYER BREAD   *4 lettuce leaves*
WITH: 4 slices bread

COVER 2ND   *4 slices Canadian bacon* (or ham)
LAYER WITH: *4 slices tomato*
                Remaining bread

Makes 4 sandwiches

• •

Mexican Chicken Sandwich

MIX: *3 oz. cream cheese,* at room temperature
                    ¼ cup olives, chopped (or more to taste)
                    Dash chili powder

SPREAD ON: *8 slices raisin bread*

ADD: *4–8 slices cooked chicken*

Makes 4 sandwiches

• •

Chicken Guacamole

MIX: *1 avocado,* mashed
                    1 Tb. lime juice (or lemon)
                    1 Tb. chopped onion
                    2 Tbs. mayonnaise

FILL: *8 frankfurter rolls* with mixture

ADD: *1 cup cooked chicken,* chopped
                    ½ cup lettuce, shredded

Makes 8 rolls

• •

Curried Chicken Sandwich

MIX:
    1 cup cooked chicken, chopped
    ¼ cup mayonnaise
    1 tsp. curry powder (or more to taste)
    ¼ lb. seedless grapes (if they are large, cut them in half)

SPREAD ON:
    8 biscuits

Makes 8 small sandwiches

• •

Turkey Sandwich

SPREAD:
    8 slices white bread with:
    Butter

ADD:
    8 slices turkey (2 to each sandwich)
    1 cup leftover stuffing, moistened with:
    Red wine (or sour cream)

Variation:
    Omit stuffing and use cranberry-orange relish

Makes 4 sandwiches

• •

Salami and Blue Cheese Sandwich

MIX:
    ½ stick butter, at room temperature
    2 oz. blue cheese

SPREAD ON: *8 slices pumpernickel*

ADD: *8 slices salami*
                4 lettuce leaves

Makes 4 sandwiches

• •

Liverwurst Sandwich

MIX: *8 slices liverwurst,* mashed with fork
                2 Tbs. chopped onion
                1 Tb. prepared mustard
                Mayonnaise to taste

SPREAD ON: *4 slices pumpernickel*

ADD: *Lettuce leaves*
                4 slices pumpernickel

Makes 4 sandwiches

• •

Spicy Bologna Sandwich

MIX: *1 pkg. (3 oz.) cream cheese,* at room temperature

                2 Tbs. prepared horseradish

SPREAD ON: *8 slices rye bread*

ADD: *8 slices bologna* (or Lebanon bologna if available)

                1 onion, sliced very thin

Makes 4 sandwiches

• •

Caviar Sandwich

SPREAD: *8 slices pumpernickel* with:
           Butter (or cream cheese), at room temperature

ADD: *1 can (4½ oz.) liver paté* (preferably im-
           ported), sliced thin
           1 small onion, sliced paper-thin
           Sprinkling of black caviar (the inexpensive kind
           is fine)

Makes 4 sandwiches

• •

"Novie" Sandwich

SPREAD: *8 slices rye bread* (thin-sliced preferred) with:
           1 pkg. (3 oz.) cream cheese

ADD: *8 slices smoked Nova Scotia Salmon* (from del-
           icatessen), 2 slices per sandwich
           1 small onion, sliced paper-thin

Variations: In place of cream cheese and onion, use butter,
           sliced tomatoes, capers and a dash of lemon;
           or substitute cottage cheese for the cream
           cheese and diet rye bread, for the dieter

Makes 4 sandwiches

• •

Sardine Sandwich

SPREAD: *8 slices white bread* with:
               Butter (or mayonnaise)

ADD: *1 can (4³⁄₈ oz.) sardines*
               2 hard-boiled eggs, sliced
               8 lettuce leaves

Makes 4 sandwiches

• •

Shellfish Sandwich

MIX: *1 cup cooked shellfish* (lobster, shrimp, or crab-
               meat)
               ½ cup mayonnaise
               1 chopped egg
               1 tsp. each chopped chives and capers

SPREAD IN: *Hamburger buns* (or frankfurter rolls)

Variations: Omit egg, and add ¼ cup chili sauce and 1 Tb.
               chopped parsley; or substitute cottage cheese
               for the mayonnaise and diet bread for the
               rolls to make low-cal sandwiches

Makes 4–6 sandwiches

• •

Tuna-Apple Sandwich

MIX: *1 can (7 oz.) tuna fish*, drained and flaked with
                a fork
                Mayonnaise to taste
                2 apples, peeled and chopped
                2 celery stalks, chopped
                Prepared mustard to taste

FILL: *Frankfurter rolls*

Variation: Omit celery and mustard, and add ½ cup
                chopped nuts and curry powder to taste

Makes 4–6 sandwiches

• •

Herring Sandwich

MIX: *1 jar (8 oz.) herring in sour cream*
                4 oz. (1¼ can) sliced new potatoes

FILL: *Pumpernickel*, lined with
                Lettuce leaves

Makes 4–8 sandwiches (depending on desired thickness)

• •

Seasoned Sandwich Butters

CREAM: ½ stick butter, at room temperature

MIX WITH ANY OF THE FOLLOWING:

1-2 Tbs. anchovy paste, 1 Tb. minced onion

2 Tbs. minced parsley, dash lemon

4 Tbs. grated Parmesan cheese, 1 tsp. garlic salt

2 tsps. dry mustard, 1 tsp. finely chopped pickles

1 Tb. Worcestershire sauce, 1 Tb. chopped onion

1 Tb. horseradish, 1 tsp. minced onion

2 Tbs. chopped parsley, 1 minced garlic clove

2 Tbs. finely chopped green pepper, 1 radish, finely chopped

• •

Seasoned Sandwich Spreads

CREAM: 1 pkg. (3 oz.) cream cheese, at room temperature

MIX WITH ANY OF THE FOLLOWING:

3 oz. blue cheese, 3 Tbs. brandy

2 Tbs. sherry, 1 tsp. Worcestershire sauce, garlic salt

1 Tb. horseradish, 1 Tb. chopped onion

2 Tbs. chili sauce, dash lemon (for seafood)

2 Tbs. chutney, 1 tsp. curry powder

2 Tbs. finely chopped nuts

4 Tbs. stuffed olives, finely chopped

• •

Seasoned Sandwich Fillings

MIX: 2 hard-boiled eggs, chopped fine
                       Mayonnaise, enough to moisten well

COMBINE WITH ANY OF THE FOLLOWING:

1 tsp. prepared mustard, canned French Fried
   Onion Rings, crumbled
Diced Muenster cheese, crumbled bacon
1 tsp. anchovy paste, 1 Tb. capers
1 Tb. each chives, chopped parsley, chopped
   celery
Curry powder to taste, 4 Tbs. minced shrimp

7

FRIENDLY
SIDEKICKS

A friendly sidekick—appetizer, salad, vegetable, or bread—
should be a good companion for the entrée, and the dessert should
complement the entire meal. The best chefs plan the entire menu
with great care, considering nutrition, variety of textures, even
contrasting colors. While I don't intend to cover the entire palette
—or palate, for that matter—nor give basic instructions on how
to slice a tomato, this chapter gives suggestions for unusual
accompaniments to round out a meal.

When we are on the move, traveling a good distance each day,
I generally rely on the main dish and serve a large tossed salad
and store-bought dessert. But when there's more time, or when I
am packing up for an outing away from home, I find a special
hors d'oeuvre, side-dish, or dessert welcome for morale as well
as nutrition.

The recipes in this chapter are meant for all the kinds of travel
life in the cookbook—some are to pack at home and serve .t
picnics or special outings, some for the campstove, and some for
the grill. The common denominators for all are ease, convenience,
or "packability" . . . and taste.

APPETIZER DIPS

Easy To Do: all of the following hors d'oeuvres are quickly prepared at home or at camp, and are best served with assorted
crackers and raw vegetables. A selection of sliced cucumbers and
carrots, celery, cauliflowerets, mushrooms, cherry tomatoes, brus-
sels sprouts, and scallions will please dieters and help balance the
menu.

Guacamole Dip

MASH: *1 peeled ripe avocado,* reserving pit

ADD: *Juice 1 lime* (or lemon)
               2 Tbs. minced onion
               1 tsp. pepper, mix thoroughly, and place the pit
                  in the dip until ready to serve—it will keep
                  the avocado from discoloring!

• •

Caviar Dip

MIX: *1 cup sour cream*
               2 minced garlic cloves (or garlic powder, not
                  salt)
               4 Tbs. black caviar (the inexpensive kind is
                  fine, but the dip will be a greyish color)

• •

Cocktail Sauce

MIX:

½ cup ketchup
Juice ½ lime
1–2 Tbs. prepared horseradish—we like it hot!

• •

Low-cal Dip

MIX:

1 pkg. (8 oz.) cottage cheese
1 small onion, minced
2 Tbs. blue cheese

• •

Sauce Verte

MIX:

1 cup mayonnaise (or half mayonnaise, half sour cream)
1 Tb. each chopped parsley, chives, tarragon, dill
2 Tbs. chopped cooked spinach (optional)—this is the standard ingredient but a nuisance unless you are serving spinach with the rest of the meal
1 tsp. garlic salt

• •

Brandied Blue Cheese

MIX:

 4 oz. blue cheese, at room temperature
 3 oz. cream cheese, at room temperature
 2 Tbs. brandy (or rum, bourbon, sherry—whatever is at hand)

• •

OTHER APPETIZERS

Baby Shrimp Hors d'Oeuvres

MIX:

 3 Tbs. mayonnaise
 1 tsp. dry mustard
 1 can (4½ oz.) baby shrimp, drained and rinsed

SPREAD ON: *Ritz crackers,* just before serving

• •

Smoked Salmon Hors d'Oeuvres

SPREAD: *Party Rye Bread* (or pumpernickel) with:
 Cream cheese, at room temperature

TOP WITH: *Thin-sliced onion*
 Smoked Nova Scotia salmon (or lox)
 Capers (optional)

• •

Southern Shrimp

MODERATE TIME: this should be made several days ahead of time, and is best for a large group; although it looks soupy, it tastes magnificent.

MARINATE: *1 pkg. (8 oz.) cooked shrimp* in:
                     1 cup vegetable oil
                     1 cup ketchup
                     ¼ cup vinegar
                     1 large onion, sliced paper thin, place in tightly covered jar and refrigerate

Before serving: Bring to room temperature, stir frequently and serve on Triscuits

• •

Steak Tartare in Mushroom Caps

FILL: *Mushroom caps* (the largest you can find), with:
                    Steak Tartare, p. 96

SPRINKLE   *Minced parsley*
WITH: *Black caviar* (optional)

N.B.—Hot Meatballs (p. 119) are also a marvelous appetizer for a large gathering.

• •

Cold Cut Roll Ups

SPREAD: *Salami,* sliced very thin, with:
               Cream cheese
               Horseradish (use sparingly!); roll and secure
                  with toothpicks

SPREAD: *Bologna,* sliced thin, with:
               Blue cheese, at room temperature, roll and se-
                  cure with toothpicks

SPREAD: *Lebanon bologna* with:
               Cream cheese, roll and secure with toothpicks

Before serving:

               Slice rolls crosswise, ½ inch thick

• •

Melon and Proscuitto

WRAP: *Melon balls* (thaw and drain if frozen) in:
               Thin-sliced prosciutto (or boiled ham), and se-
                  cure with toothpicks

• •

Toothpick Skewers

SPEAR:

Cheese cubes (cut about ½ inch thick)
Assorted cold cut cubes
Cherry tomatoes
Cocktail onions
Olives
Gherkins, making a variety of combinations on
toothpicks

• •

Marinated Mushrooms

DRAIN: *1 jar (4½ oz.) mushroom caps*

FILL JAR   *Vinegar*, halfway to top of jar
WITH: *Water*, almost to top
                1 garlic clove, peeled
                1 Tb. basil (or tarragon), and replace lid
                tightly

CHILL: 1 hour or more (these will keep several weeks)
                and serve with toothpicks for very low-cal
                appetizer

• •

Cucumber Appetizers

SPREAD: *Party Rye Bread* (or pumpernickel) with:
                1 pkg. cream cheese and chives

ADD: *Thin slices cucumber*
                 Fresh chopped chives (if available)

• •

Pickle Rolls

WRAP: *Large dill pickles* in:
                 Thin-sliced dried beef (packaged) spread with:
                 Cream cheese

Before serving:

                 Slice crosswise, ¼ inch thick

• •

New Potato Appetizer

MODERATE TIME: these make a delicious and elaborate first course
or vegetable for a light tailgate spread.

BOIL: *New potatoes* 15–20 minutes, until just done,
                     drain and scoop out a third of each potato

FILL WITH: *Salt*
                 Minced onion
                 Sour cream
                 Black caviar, wrap and serve warm if possible

(N.B.—an empty egg carton is perfect for packing the new
potatoes)

SALADS

Artichoke Salad

MIX: *1 can (15 oz.) artichoke hearts,* drained and rinsed
                1 clove garlic, minced (or garlic powder)
                6 Tbs. olive oil
                2 Tbs. vinegar
                Salt, pepper to taste

TOSS WITH: *1 head Boston lettuce,* torn into small pieces

Serves 4–6

• •

Asparagus Salad

MIX: *½ cup mayonnaise*
                1 hard-boiled egg, mashed with a fork
                Garlic salt, pepper to taste

SERVE ON: *1 can (15 oz.) asparagus spears,* rinsed and drained
                Lettuce leaves

Serves 4

• •

Boston Lettuce Salad

MIX:
> *1 tsp. sugar*
> *2 Tbs. olive oil*
> *Juice ½ lemon*

ADD:
> *1 small head Boston lettuce,* rinsed and only
> slightly drained

Serves 2

• •

Carrot-raisin Salad

SHRED:
> *1 lb. carrots,* washed and scraped

ADD:
> *1 cup raisins*
> *Mayonnaise* to taste

Serves 4

• •

Cucumber Dill Salad

SLICE:
> *2 large cucumbers,* peeled, very thin, and sprin-
> kle each layer with:
> *Garlic salt;* let stand ½ hour or more

SQUEEZE:
> Cucumbers until limp, and drain

ADD: *1 Tb. vinegar*
                4 Tbs. sour cream
                2 Tbs. dill weed (fresh dill preferred), and toss
                   lightly

Serves 4

• •

Cole Slaw with Apples

MIX: *1 small head cabbage,* shredded
                2 apples, peeled and diced
                ¾ cup mayonnaise
                Raisins, chopped nuts (optional)

Serves 4

• •

Green Pepper-tomato Salad

BOIL: *2 green peppers,* thinly sliced, until just tender;
                   drain

SPRINKLE   *Olive oil*
WITH: *Vinegar*
                Garlic salt, pepper

ADD: *1 small onion,* thinly sliced
                3 large tomatoes, thinly sliced, and toss lightly

Serves 4

• •

Onion Tomato Salad

MIX: *1 Tb. olive oil*
            3 Tbs. vinegar
            1 tsp. garlic salt
            3 large Beefsteak tomatoes, sliced
            1 red onion, sliced paper thin, and toss

Serves 4

• •

Tomato Mushroom Salad

MIX: *2 Tbs. olive oil*
            2 Tbs. vinegar
            3 Beefsteak tomatoes, chopped coarsely
            ¼ lb. fresh mushrooms, washed and sliced
            Garlic salt, pepper

Serves 4

• •

Marinated Green Beans

MIX: *1 can (16 oz.) green beans,* drained and rinsed
            ½ tsp. garlic salt, pepper
            Dash olive oil
            4 Tbs. vinegar, and chill 1 hour if possible

SERVE ON: *Lettuce leaves (optional)*

Variation: Substitute slightly undercooked fresh string
                 beans or frozen beans for a much better but
                 not as quick dish

Serves 2–3

• •

Eggplant Sticks

MODERATE TIME: these make a marvelous dish to serve cold as
finger food in the car or on a picnic, or hot off the campstove.

SLICE: *1 medium eggplant,* peeled, into long, ½ inch
                fingers
DREDGE IN: *Evaporated milk,* then in:
                Bread crumbs
SAUTÉ IN: ½ *stick butter,* over fairly high heat, turning
                once, until tender and golden (add more butter
                if necessary); drain on paper towels
Variation: For a lighter dish, substitute flour for the milk
                and bread crumbs

Serves 4

• •

Ratatouille

ELABORATE: this takes quite a while to cook, but it will keep a
week or so in the refrigerator or may be made up more quickly
in smaller quantities on the campstove; either hot or cold, it is
an extraordinary dish.

SAUTÉ:	*2 onions,* sliced thin
	2 garlic cloves, minced, in:
	¼ *cup olive oil,* until lightly browned
ADD:	*1 medium eggplant,* cut in small cubes
	4 small zucchini, sliced ¼ inch thick
	2 green peppers, cut in thin strips; more oil if needed
SIMMER:	20 minutes, covered, stirring occasionally
ADD:	*4 tomatoes,* diced
	Capers or sliced olives (optional)
SIMMER:	10 minutes, covered, and serve hot or chilled

Serves 8

• •

Vegetables à la Grecque

HEAT:	¼ *cup olive oil*
	Juice of 1 lemon
	1 garlic clove, minced
	1 tsp. each salt, pepper, tarragon, parsley
ADD:	*3 cups assorted chopped vegetables:* celery, mushrooms, white onions, green pepper, eggplant, artichoke hearts, cauliflower, zucchini, green beans, or scallions, and stir to coat with oil mixture
ADD:	*Water,* just enough to cover vegetables, cover and simmer on low heat until crisp (about 15 minutes). Chill in the liquid

Serves 6

• •

Marinated Onions

SLICE: *3 large, red onions,* paper thin, and place in jar
ADD: *4 Tbs. olive oil*
              2 Tbs. vinegar
              4 Tbs. wine
              1/2 tsp. sugar
              1 pkg. (3 oz.) blue cheese, crumbled, and chill
                  several days if possible
SERVE WITH: Lettuce leaves, crackers or pumpernickel bread

Serves 6

• •

Spinach Salad I

MIX: *2 Tbs. lemon juice* (or vinegar)
              6 Tbs. olive oil
              1 Tb. sugar
              Salt, pepper
              1 pkg. (10 oz.) fresh spinach, trimmed carefully
                  and torn into small pieces
              2 hard-boiled eggs (optional), sliced
              1/4 lb. fresh mushrooms (optional), sliced

Serves 4–6

• •

Spinach Salad II

—for camping or boating, not picnicking, since bacon must be hot.

FRY: *4 slices bacon,* and drain on towel, saving bacon
       fat

MIX: *¼ cup bacon fat*
       Juice 1 lemon
       ½ tsp. sugar (or more to taste)
       Garlic salt, pepper
       1 pkg. (10 oz.) spinach, trimmed carefully and
       torn into small pieces

ADD: Bacon, crumbled, and toss before serving

Serves 4

• •

Garbanzo Salad

MIX: *4 Tbs. olive oil*
       2 Tbs. vinegar
       1 tsp. garlic salt, pepper
       1 medium onion, chopped fine
       1 large tomato, chopped fine
       1 can (1 lb. 4 oz.) garbanzos (chick peas),
       drained and rinsed; marinate 1 hour or more
       if possible

Serves 4

• •

Kidney Bean Salad

MIX:
    2 cans (1 lb. each) red kidney beans, drained and rinsed
    1 cup diced cucumbers (peeled)
    1 cup diced celery
    ½ cup chopped green pepper
    ½ cup chopped Bermuda onion
    Salt, pepper
    Mayonnaise to taste, and let stand several hours if possible

Serves 4–6

• •

German Potato Salad

MIX:
    1 can (1 lb.) sliced new potatoes, drained and rinsed
    3 Tbs. vinegar
    2 Tbs. olive oil
    Garlic salt, pepper, chives
    ½ cucumber, peeled and diced
    1 small onion, chopped fine

ADD:
    Mayonnaise to taste
    2 Tbs. capers (optional)

Serves 3

• •

Potato Salad Dumas

MIX: 2 Tbs. white wine
                     2 Tbs. vinegar
                     3 Tbs. olive oil
                     Salt, pepper
                     1 can (1 lb.) sliced new potatoes, drained and
                         rinsed
                     2 Tbs. each chopped parsley, chives
                     1 cup mussels (canned or bottled)

Serves 3

● ●

Cold Rice Salad

MIX: 2 cups cooked rice
                     4 Tbs. vinegar
                     6–8 Tbs. olive oil
                     2 cloves garlic, minced (or garlic salt)
                     1 small onion, chopped fine
                     2 tomatoes, diced
                     ¼ cup chopped parsley

Serves 6

● ●

SOUPS

Avocado Soup

EASY TO DO: but must be prepared at home

BLEND:
>3 cups water
>3 chicken bouillon cubes
>1 ripe avocado, diced
>Juice 1 lime
>Pepper, to taste; chill and pack in thermos bottle

Serves 4

• •

Cold Cucumber Soup

ELABORATE: this delicious soup must be prepared ahead of time,
at home.

SAUTÉ:
>1 medium onion, sliced thin, in:
>1 Tb. olive oil, until soft

ADD:
>2 large cucumbers, diced but not peeled
>1 tsp. cornstarch, blended with a little water
>2 cups chicken bouillon
>Salt, pepper

SIMMER:
>20 minutes, cool and blend until smooth in small
>batches in automatic blender

ADD:
>1 cup cream
>½ cup dry vermouth, chill and pack in thermos
>bottle

Serves 6

• •

Curried Chicken Soup

Easy To Do: this can be prepared in minutes at home or camp-site.

MIX: *1 can (10½ oz.) cream of chicken soup*
      1 can milk
      1–2 tsps. curry powder, stir well and chill or
      serve immediately

Serves 4

• •

Gazpacho

Moderate Time: this marvelous Spanish salad-in-a-soup requires some chopping and an automatic blender, but it's low calorie and highly refreshing.

CHOP   *2 cloves garlic*
COARSELY: *4 tomatoes,* peeled
              1 cucumber, peeled
              1 onion, peeled
              1 green pepper, seeded

ADD: *4 raw eggs,* and blend in small batches until
              smooth

STIR IN: *¼ cup vinegar*
              ¼ cup olive oil
              ¾ cup tomato juice
              Salt, pepper, chill overnight and pack in thermos
              bottle

Serves 6–8

• •

Iced Pea Soup

Easy To Do: delicious despite the too bright, bright green color.

BLEND: *1 pkg. frozen peas* (defrosted)
           1 cup chicken bouillon
           1 Tb. mint or basil
           2 Tbs. dry vermouth, chill and pack in thermos
           bottle

• •

Shrimp Soup

Easy To Do: pack this up in a thermos bottle or whip it up on the campstove for a marvelous cold-weather warmer.

HEAT: *1 can (10 oz.) frozen cream of shrimp soup,* on
           low flame, stirring until hot but not boiling

ADD: ½ *cup milk* (or water)
           ¼ *cup sherry*
           2 oz. cheese—grated Parmesan or shredded
           Swiss—and stir until hot

Variation: Omit milk (or water) and serve on patty shells
           or French bread for a main-dish chowder

Serves 3

• •

BREADS

Banana Bread

Easy To Do: this family favorite takes only 15 minutes to prepare for baking, and is excellent for a car trip or a special outing.

MELT: *1 stick butter* in bread loaf pan, and swirl to grease pan

BEAT: *2 eggs,* until fluffy, then add and beat:
              3 ripe bananas

ADD: *¾ cup sugar*
              1½ cups flour
              1 tsp. baking powder
              1 tsp. salt
              the melted butter, and stir until mixed

BAKE: 1 hour at 325°. (recipe may be doubled; it freezes well)

• •

Raisin Bread

Easy To Do: I clocked this at 10 minutes preparation, 1 hour baking.

MIX: *1 cup flour*
              ½ cup sugar
              2 Tbs. baking powder
              ½ tsp. salt
              ¾ cup raisins

ADD: *1 egg,* beaten with a fork
               1 cup milk, mix and pour in greased loaf pan

BAKE: 1 hour at 350°

• •

Nut Bread

EASY To Do: especially good with poultry or Chicken Salad.

MIX: *1 egg,* beaten with a fork
               1 cup milk

ADD: *2 cups flour*
               3 tsps. baking powder
               ½ cup sugar
               ½ tsp. salt
               ½ cup chopped nuts, mix thoroughly and pour
                   into greased loaf pan

BAKE: 50–60 minutes at 350°

• •

Giant Croutons

EASY To Do: these are quick, good and inordinately useful while
camping since they may be served by themselves or as a base for
meat or poultry.

MELT: *¼ stick butter* in frying pan until bubbling

ADD: *4 thick slices white bread,* crust removed, and
                   fry slowly until golden

ADD: ¼ *stick butter,* turn coutons and cook until
                golden

Variation: Serve the croutons with cinnamon sugar or maple
                syrup for breakfast

Serves 4

• •

French Toast

EASY TO DO: richer, and slightly more trouble than Giant Croutons, French Toast is as good served with supper as it is for
breakfast.

MIX: *1 egg,* beaten with a fork
                ⅔ cup milk

ADD: *6 slices thin white bread,* turning to coat with
                mixture

SAUTÉ IN: *Butter,* until golden on both sides

Serves 3–6

• •

Skillet Biscuits

EASY TO DO: it's possible to use your favorite brand of refrigerator buns and cook them while camping or boating without an
oven.

MELT: *2 Tbs. butter* in skillet

ADD: *1 pkg. refrigerator biscuits,* placing them evenly
                   around pan

COVER WITH: *Aluminum foil,* making a low tent, cook on very
                   low flame until light brown, turn, brown
                   lightly and serve immediately

● ●

Garlic Bread Slices

MELT: *Butter,* about 1 Tb. per person, and sprinkle
                   with:
                   Garlic salt

SAUTÉ: *French bread,* sliced thick, until golden on both
                   sides, adding more butter if necessary

● ●

Foiled Garlic Bread

SLICE: *1 loaf French bread* into ¾-inch-thick slices

SPREAD WITH: *1 stick butter,* at room temperature
                   Garlic salt to taste—we use lots

WRAP IN: *Aluminum foil* and warm at side of burner or
                   grill

Serves 6–8

● ●

Foiled Rye Bread

SPREAD: *8 slices rye bread* with:
                 Butter
                 Instant minced onion, and reassemble into loaf

WRAP IN: *Aluminum foil* and warm at side of burner or
                 grill

Serves 4

• •

Herb Bread

SLICE: *1 loaf French bread* lengthwise

SPREAD WITH: *1 stick butter,* at room temperature
                 Garlic salt
                 4 Tbs. chopped parsley
                 3 scallions, chopped fine

WRAP IN: *Aluminum foil,* warm at side of burner or grill,
                 and cut into thick slices

Serves 6–8

• •

Foiled Stuffing

EASY TO DO: this marvelous instant side dish for poultry or
meats may be cooked on the side of the grill or at the back of the
campstove.

PLACE: 1 cup (1 pkg.) seasoned stuffing mix (Peppe-ridge Farm recommended) on large sheet of aluminum foil, shiny side up

ADD: 1 cup water, drizzling it evenly over stuffing
1 stick butter, placing small pats evenly on stuffing, and wrap tightly in the foil

COOK: 10 minutes, until butter is melted and stuffing is hot, at side of grill or campstove

Serves 4–6

• •

DESSERTS

Meringue Kisses

EASY TO DO: vary the flavor by topping the meringues with jam or nuts.

BEAT: 3 egg whites until stiff but not dry

ADD SLOWLY: 1 cup sugar, pinch salt

FOLD IN: 1 tsp. vanilla, and drop by spoonful on greased (or Teflon) cookie sheet

BAKE: 60 minutes at 225°, or until firm

• •

Hermits

Easy To Do: these are particularly good travelers for a long trip.

BEAT: *1 stick butter,* at room temperature

ADD: *½ cup brown sugar*
          1 egg, and beat well

ADD: *1 cup flour*
          1 tsp. baking powder
          Dash nutmeg, cinnamon
          1 cup golden raisins, mix and pour into 7-inch-
          square pan

BAKE: 20–30 minutes at 350°, and cut into a dozen
          squares

• •

Strawberry Shortbread

Easy To Do: very rich and delicious, but note that this is short-
bread, not strawberry shortcake—which I also recommend!

MIX: *1 stick butter,* at room temperature, with:
          ½ cup sugar

ADD: *1 egg yolk,* and mix thoroughly

ADD: *1 cup flour,* mix and pat into greased pan (a
          5 x 7 inch aluminum foil pan, saved from
          frozen foods, can be used to bake and trans-
          port the shortbread)

BAKE: 45 minutes at 325°

ADD: *Strawberry jam,* spreading over top, and bake
          10 minutes

• •

Cinnamon Shortbread

EASY TO DO: 8 minutes preparation time, if the butter is very soft.

MIX: *1 stick butter,* very soft
                  ½ cup extra fine sugar
                  1½ cups flour
                  1 tsp. vanilla, and pour in greased 7-inch-square
                      pan, or comparable aluminum foil pan
ADD: *Cinnamon sugar,* sprinkling thickly over top
BAKE: 20 minutes at 350°

• •

Chocolate Whiffs

EASY TO DO: these meringue-like squares will deflate and look slightly odd but they taste marvelous.

BEAT: *3 egg whites* until stiff
BEAT: *3 egg yolks,* and add:
                  ½ cup sugar
                  2 Tbs. cocoa
                  1 tsp. flour
FOLD IN: Egg whites, and pour in greased aluminum foil
                      dish (approximately 6 x 8″)
BAKE: 20—30 minutes at 400°, until set but still soft

• •

Pecan Cake

MODERATE TIME: a perfect summer dessert.

BEAT:	*3 egg whites* until stiff
BEAT:	*3 egg yolks,* and add:
	½ cup sugar
	¼ cup cocoa
	1 cup ground pecans (you can do this in a blender)
	1 tsp. vanilla, and pour into greased aluminum foil pan (approximately 6 x 8 inches)
BAKE:	25 minutes at 350°, let cool and cut into squares

• •

Butterscotch Squares

EASY TO DO: rich and practical to transport for a picnic.

MELT:	*⅔ stick butter* in 7-inch pan or aluminum foil pan, swirling to grease pan
MIX:	*1 egg,* beaten with a fork
	1 tsp. baking powder
	¼ tsp. salt
	½ tsp. vanilla
	¾ cup flour
	1 cup brown sugar
ADD TO MIX:	The melted butter, and pour back in pan
BAKE:	20–25 minutes at 350°, and cut into small squares

• •

Brownies

EASY To Do: a family favorite, my daughters whip this up in no time.

MELT: ½ *stick butter* in 7" pan or aluminum foil pan, swirling to grease pan

MIX: *2 pkts. (1 oz. each) premelted chocolate* (or 2 ozs. melted unsweetened chocolate)
                2 eggs
                1 cup sugar
                ½ *cup flour*
                1 tsp. vanilla, dash salt
                Melted butter, and pour into pan

BAKE: 1 hour at 300°

• •

Sherried Rum Cake

EASY To Do: this is really an instant dessert, although it is best to assemble it a few hours ahead of time to blend the flavors; equally good when traveling, camping, or boating.

POUR: ½ *cup sherry*
                ½ *cup rum* (or combination of whatever wines and liquors are at hand), slowly on:
                1 lb. pound cake (thawed if frozen)

SPREAD WITH: *Jam* (apricot, strawberry, or currant are good choices)

SERVE WITH: *Instant whipped cream (optional)*

• •

Bourbon Balls

MODERATE TIME: it just takes awhile to form all these marble-sized balls, with no other cooking involved; they are very rich and would keep a long time in the refrigerator, but, alas, they seem to disappear.

MIX:

> *1 cup confectioner's sugar*
> *2 Tbs. cocoa mix*
> *2 cups graham cracker crumbs*
> *1 Tb. butter (optional)* at room temperature
> *¼ cup bourbon* (or rum), adding more if necessary to form a very thick dough

SHAPE:

> Bourbon mixture into very small balls (about ¾-inch)

ROLL IN:

> *Cocoa mix* (or confectioner's sugar), and let stand 24 hours if possible

• •

QUICK AND EASY FRUIT DESSERTS

EASY TO DO: all of the following desserts are marvelous to prepare while camping or to pack up at home and gobble at an outing.

Blueberries With Sour Cream

SPRINKLE: *Blueberries* with:
                Brown sugar
                Sour cream, and serve in bowls (paper bowls are fine!)

Variations: Substitute strawberries or green grapes for the blueberries

• •

Liqueured Fruits

SPRINKLE: *Blueberries with Kirsch* or
                Frozen raspberries (thawed) with Cointreau or
                Canned pear halves, drained, with Marsala or
                Canned apricot halves, drained, with Rum

• •

Strawberries in Wine

SPRINKLE: *Fresh strawberries,* sliced, with:
                Sugar, and let stand ½ hour to bring out juices

ADD: *White wine* (about ½ cup per pint)

Variation: Substitute fresh, sliced peaches and brown sugar for the strawberries and sugar

• •

Ambrosia Cup

MIX: *Sliced bananas*
                Canned pineapple chunks (or tropical fruits)
                Sliced strawberries
                Canned Mandarin oranges (or fresh orange sec-
                    tions)
                Grated coconut
                Kirsch (optional)

• •

Instant Strawberry Shortcake

FILL: *Dessert patty shells* (or top sliced pound cake)
                    with:
                Frozen strawberries (thawed) with juice
TOP WITH: *Instant whipped cream*
Variations: Substitute fresh blueberries or sliced peaches
                    (fresh or frozen) for the strawberries

• •

Friut and Cheese Dessert

COMBINE: *Munster cheese* and
                Golden Delicious apple wedges
                Blue cheese and
                Fresh pears, quartered
                Cheddar cheese cubes and
                Grapes

• •

Peach Melba

DRAIN :   *1 can (1 lb. 14 oz.) peach halves*
FILL WITH :   *Vanilla ice cream*
TOP WITH :   *1 cup raspberry jam,* hot or at room temperature

● ●

Apricots with Jam

DRAIN :   *1 can (16 oz.) apricot halves* (or pears)
FILL WITH :   *Strawberry jam*
TOP WITH :   *Instant whipped cream*
Variation :   Substitute peaches and raspberry jam for the
                   apricots and strawberry jam

● ●

QUICK TRICKS

EASY TO DO: the following appeal particularly to the young, and
are ready in seconds.

Kiddie Bags

MIX:

M & Ms (candy)
Raisins
Nuts, and pack in individual plastic bags for a
neat, energy-giving dessert snack

• •

S'Mores

BROIL:

Marshmallows over charcoal fire, and place between:
Chocolate Wafers (or vanilla wafers)—have lots
of cookies and marshmallows, since the name
of this comes from always wanting some more

Variation:

Substitute the following chocolate sauce for the
cookies, and dip the marshmallows in it

• •

Instant Chocolate Sauce

MIX:

¼ cup milk
½ cup cocoa mix, and serve hot or cold on ice
cream or cake

Variation:

For an Instant Banana Split, serve on sliced
bananas and ice cream and top with Instant
Whipped Cream

• •

8

BACK TO THE BASICS

Meat Marinades

MIX:

½ *cup olive oil*
1 garlic clove, minced
1 onion, chopped finely
1 Tb. each parsley, oregano (optional)
½ *cup sherry*

MIX:

1 tsp. garlic salt
½ *tsp. pepper*
¼ *cup olive oil*
½ *cup dry red wine*

MIX:

½ *cup soy sauce*
½ *cup white wine*
1 garlic clove, minced
1 tsp. powdered ginger
1 tsp. sugar (optional)

MIX:

¼ *cup soy sauce*
¼ *cup ketchup*
¼ *cup vinegar*
1 Tb. brown sugar

Enough for 4 servings

• •

Fish Marinades

MIX: *4 Tbs. olive oil*
                ½ cup dry vermouth
                Basil (or tarragon)

MIX: *¼ cup white wine*
                ¼ cup olive oil
                Juice 1 lemon
                2 Tbs. chopped parsley

MIX: *¼ cup white wine* (or sherry)
                ¼ cup soy sauce
                ¼ cup olive oil
                Ginger, garlic powder

• •

Vegetable Marinades

MIX: *½ cup vinegar*
                ¼ cup olive oil
                2 garlic cloves, peeled
                Salt, pepper

MIX: *½ cup olive oil*
                ¼ cup dry wine
                ¼ cup vinegar
                Garlic salt, pepper, tarragon

Enough for 4 servings

• •

SALAD DRESSINGS AND SAUCES

French Dressing

MIX:

6 Tbs. olive oil

1 tsp. garlic salt, pepper

1 Tb. tarragon, stirring with spoon in bottom of bowl

ADD:

2–3 Tbs. wine vinegar, and mix into olive oil

• •

Chilean Cocktail Sauce

MIX:

2 scallions, chopped

2 sprigs parsley, chopped

1 Tb. each tarragon, chives

¼ cup each fresh lemon juice, vinegar, white wine

Dash Tabasco, beat, chill and serve with seafood

Variation:

For piquant salad dressing, add:

2 hard-boiled eggs, finely chopped

• •

Russian Dressing

MIX:
1 cup mayonnaise
¼ cup chili sauce
1 tsp. minced onion or horseradish

Enough for 4 servings

• •

MEAT SAUCES AND GRAVIES

Mushroom Sauce

BOIL:
¾ cup water
1 beef bouillon cube (or instant bouillon)
1 Tb. instant minced onion
1 can (8 oz.) mushrooms, drained, for 10 minutes

ADD:
¼ cup Madeira (or dry red wine)
2 Tbs. butter, swirling until just melted

Enough for 4 servings

• •

Currant Gravy

MELT:
½ cup currant jelly on low heat

ADD:
½ tsp. prepared mustard
½ cup dry red wine
Juice of ½ lemon, and stir until hot

Variation: Substitute the juice and slivered rind of one
                 orange for the lemon juice and mustard

● ●

Mint Sauce

MELT: ½ *cup mint jelly* on low heat
ADD: ½ *cup water*
             ½ *tsp. instant chicken bouillon,* and stir until
             hot

Enough for 4 servings

● ●

SAUCES FOR FISH AND RAW VEGETABLES

Sauce Verte

MIX: *1 cup mayonnaise*
             2 Tbs. chopped spinach (or watercress)
             2 Tbs. each chopped parsley, chives, dill weed,
             tarragon

● ●

Sauce Rémoulade

MIX:
> *1 cup mayonnaise*
> *2 small pickles,* finely chopped
> *1 Tb. each prepared mustard, capers, chopped parsley*
> *1 hard-boiled egg (optional),* chopped

Enough for 4 servings

• •

Horseradish Sauce

MIX:
> *1 cup sour cream*
> *2 tsps. prepared horseradish*
> *1 tsp. dill weed*

Enough for 4 servings

• •

Cocktail Sauce

MIX:
> *1 cup ketchup*
> *2–4 Tbs. prepared horseradish* (we like it hot!)
> *Juice of* ½ *lime* (or lemon)

Enough for 4 servings

• •

Low-cal Sauce

MIX: *8 oz. cottage cheese*
                2 Tbs. each chopped onion, crumbled blue cheese

Enough for 4 servings

• •

COLD BEVERAGES

EASY TO DO: to be served in place of or after your favorite cocktails, these drinks are fairly light, inexpensive, and great for a
crowd.

Champagne Punch

PACK IN   *½ gallon dry, white wine* (inexpensive is fine)
ICE CHEST: *1 qt. ginger ale*
                1 bottle dry champagne (inexpensive is fine)
                1 pt. fresh strawberries (optional), sliced
                Block of ice (we make our own in a bowl in the
                    freezer)

Before serving:

                Pour all the above into large bowl, and mix

Makes 1 gallon

• •

Sangria

PACK IN ONE-
GALLON THER-
MOS BOTTLE:

2 qts. dry red wine (inexpensive, slightly harsh
    variety is preferred)
1 orange, sliced thinly, but not peeled
½ lemon, sliced thinly
1 qt. soda water, left open for an hour so it will
    go flat (and not pop the thermos bottle)
Dash of brandy (optional)
Ice cubes

Makes 3 quarts

• •

Wine Spritzer

PACK IN
ICE CHEST:

½ gallon dry white wine (inexpensive Chablis
    preferred)
1 qt. soda water
Ice cubes

TO SERVE:

Fill glasses two-thirds full with ice and wine,
    and top with soda water

Makes 3 quarts

• •

HOT BEVERAGES

EASY To Do: these may be made while camping or brewed at home and packed in a thermos bottle.

Cinnamon Coffee

BOIL: *4 cups water*
               6 Tbs. instant coffee
               4 cinnamon sticks, and serve with one stick in
                    each cup
ADD: *Sugar* to taste

Serves 4

• •

Irish Coffee

PREPARE: *4 cups strong instant coffee*
MIX: *4 tsps. sugar*
               4 oz. Irish whiskey
DIVIDE: *Irish whiskey and sugar mixture* equally in 4
                    cups
ADD: *Hot coffee*
               Instant whipped cream
               Sugar to taste

Serves 4

• •

Cinnamon Cocoa

PREPARE: *4 cups cocoa,* according to package directions

ADD: *4 cinnamon sticks*
Instant whipped cream

Serves 4

• •

INDEX